FAVORITE CHEESE RECIPES

Editorial Director	Arthur Hettich

Editor	Nancy H. Fitzpatrick
Art Director	Philip Sykes
Art Associate	Martin Silverman
Food Consultant	Lois Cristofano

All recipes tested in Family Circle's Test Kitchens.

Family Circle gratefully acknowledges the help of the United Dairy Industry Association and its operating arms—The American Dairy Association, Dairy Research Inc., and National Dairy Council—in providing background information for this guide.

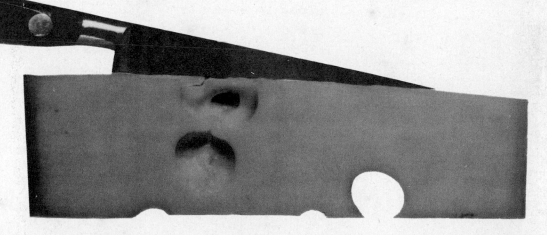

Created by Family Circle Magazine and published 1979 by Arno Press Inc., a subsidiary of The New York Times Company. Copyright © 1975 by The Family Circle, Inc. All rights reserved. Protected under Berne and other international copyright conventions. Title and Trademark FAMILY CIRCLE registered U.S. Patent and Trademark Office, Canada, Great Britain, Australia, New Zealand, Japan and other countries. Marca Registrada. This volume may not be reproduced in whole or in part in any form without written permission from the publisher. Printed in U.S.A. Library of Congress Catalog Card Number 78-68628. ISBN 0-405-12051-6.

A New York Times Company Publication

CONTENTS

1
THE CHEESE-SHOP GUIDE

People all over the world love cheese. Mainly because it tastes terrific. But partly because it's nutritious. In a concentrated form, cheese has almost all the protein, essential minerals, vitamins and other nutrients of milk. Versatility makes cheese popular, too, being as welcome on an appetizer tray as it is in a sandwich, main dish, soup, salad or dessert. Following is a guide to some of the more popular varieties of cheese, along with a bit of history, tips on buying, storing, cooking and serving this delicious food. Then, beginning with Chapter 2, you'll find recipes to please you...and all the cheese lovers you know!

It was a long time ago in a faraway Asian land. A lonely traveler set out across the dessert on his camel with a few belongings and some food, including a sheep's pouch filled with fresh milk. At nightfall, when he stopped to rest, the shepherd opened the pouch—only to discover that the milk had changed. The heat of the day, combined with the movement of travel and the rennet lining in the pouch, had separated the milk into a mixture of curds (custard-like lumps) and whey (the remaining liquid). Fortunately, the shepherd was not intimidated by the change. He drank the whey to quench his thirst and ate the curds, which not only satisfied his hunger but had a delightful taste. According to the legend, the shepherd accidentally had discovered cheese.

Today, it's no accident that cheese is one of our most popular foods. Thousands of years have been devoted to its development so that we now have hundreds of flavors, textures, sizes and shapes to choose from.

Our own American-made cheeses tell much about this history. Some have foreign-sounding names and long histories; other varieties are uniquely American, but all are a tribute to man's continual curiosity and pursuit of perfection.

Let's take a look at a few of our most popular natural cheeses and the history behind them.

Originally, the art of cheesemaking was brought here by immigrants from many parts of Europe. But it was not until the 19th century that this art moved from the family farm to local factories, the first being located near Rome, New York. The main cheese produced in this factory was Cheddar, named for Cheddar, England, where it was first made in the 16th century.

Cheddar is today the most popular of all our natural cheeses and is available in a wide range of sizes and shapes, and from mild to very sharp in flavor. The list of Cheddar names is varied, too, and includes Monterey Jack (named for Monterey, California), Longhorn, Coon and Herkimer, which was named after Herkimer County, New York.

Of course, Cheddar is just one of the basic cheese families. There are about 18 in all, including 3 popular American originals, Brick, Cream Cheese and Liederkranz. By the time one adds up all the variations within each group, the list runs into more than 800 names.

Swiss is another favorite with Americans. It was first made here by Swiss-born settlers who had migrated westward in search of good farmland. They settled in what later became Wisconsin which, today, makes the major portion of the more than 2 billion pounds of cheese we produce each year.

The holes in Swiss (gas holes produced during curing) may give the impression that something's missing. But one taste and you know nothing's been left out in the way of flavor!

Wisconsin is also credited with having produced one of the biggest cheeses in history. In 1934 a factory in Denmark, Wisconsin, produced a Goliath weighing 2,100 pounds. It was exhibited all over the country in a specially built glass refrigerator on wheels. This mammoth was later outdone by one which weighed 5,210 pounds!

To look on the small side of things for a moment, Americans also love Liederkranz, a U.S. original that's only made in 4-ounce rectangular shaped loaves. Many people erroneously think of this piquant cheese as foreign-made, but it was first produced in New York. Cheesemaker Emil Frey had set out to duplicate one of his favorite German cheeses, but ended up instead with what was to become Liederkranz—which he named after a singing society to which he belonged. Today this surface-ripened cheese is made in the Middle West.

Going further west, one discovers such cheeses as Monterey Jack, named for the town of Monterey, California, where it was first made.

But all cheeses are not named for geographic areas or sentimental reasons (as with Emil's Liederkranz). Some take their names from their shapes and sizes. Brick, for instance, is named for either its shape or for the bricks used to press the whey out of the unripened cheese during its manufacture.

As you'll notice on pages 6 and 8, we include many other popular varieties, along with information on how to identify cheeses by texture and flavor. Plus there's more about the history and lore behind the names and the development of this wonderful food.

THE NATURAL CHEESES

On this and the next three pages you'll find 26 popular natural cheeses, some of the history behind them, information on flavors and textures, as well as specific serving suggestions. Then, on pages 10 and 11 we include descriptions of still other varieties. All in all, this guide is designed to make you familiar with some of our finest cheeses.

1 **CHEDDAR** is a hard cheese with a smooth, firm body. Made from sweet whole cow's milk, it ranges from mild to medium to sharp in flavor depending upon its aging; and in color, from nearly white to orange. Its shape is varied, too, including wheels, wedges, cylinders, loaves, bricks, rectangles, pineapples, barrels and tubes. But no matter how you slice it or eat it (cooked, on sandwiches, in salads or pie), it's delicious.

The origin of this cheese begins in 16th century Somerset, England, in a village named, appropriately, Cheddar. When it emigrated to the United States, it became known as Cheddar-American, American Cheddar, or simply American cheese. Today, we have as many as 25 types of Cheddar, including Colby, Monterey Jack, Longhorn, Coon, Kuminost and Herkimer.

2 **MONTEREY JACK** was first made about 1892 by monks in Monterey, California. It's a variety of Cheddar that has a smooth, somewhat open texture. Depending on the milk and the aging, it can range from semisoft to hard. Monterey Jack is similar to Colby in taste and is white to light cream in color. Try it on sandwiches, in salads, to eat out of hand, or for use in cooking.

3 **WHITE CHEDDAR** is usually hard, with a somewhat crumbly texture (see Cheddar). And its taste is distinctively sharp—a delightful attribute when you want a real cheesy flavor in casseroles.

4 **GOUDA** was first made in the vicinity of Gouda, in the Province of South Holland. This creamy yellow sweet-curd cheese has a mild to medium nut-like flavor; and is semisoft to hard in texture. Similar to Edam, the cheese is known for its spherical shape, and usually comes with a yellow or red wax coating. Serve it on crackers, with fruit or shredded in omelets. Note: The Gouda shown is Caraway Gouda.

5 **LARGE EDAM.** This cheese is readily identifiable by its creamy yellow color, flaming red coating and cellophane-type wrapper. Popularly called the red cannonball, it was first made in the North of Holland in the 16th century. Today, in Wisconsin alone, about 2 million pounds of Edam are produced annually, a good indication of its ever-growing popularity. Edam has a mild, nutlike flavor and an open body.

6 **SMALL EDAM** is packaged with the same red coating as the large Edam (see above), but on a smaller, conveniently-sized scale.

7 **COTTAGE CHEESE** is a soft, uncured cheese sometimes called pot cheese or Dutch cheese. Made from skim milk, it comes packaged in cup-like containers in either creamed or dry form, with moist large or small curds. The mild, slightly acid flavor of this cheese makes it adaptable to a wide variety of uses, including salads, main dishes, cheesecakes, sandwiches, and with fruits and vegetables. It's economical, low in calories and nutritious. Since it is a fresh cheese, cottage cheese should be used soon after purchase.

8 **CREAM CHEESE.** This is an American original, first made in 1872, and today enjoyed as one of our most popular soft cheeses. Made from cream or a mixture of cream and milk, it has a smooth, buttery texture and a delicate flavor, making it perfect for spreading on sandwiches, mixing in dips, salad dressings and cheesecakes. Cream cheese is a fresh cheese and should be used soon after purchase.

9 **FARM OR FARMER CHEESE.** Sometimes called pressed or pot cheese, this is a white, dry cottage cheese pressed into small rectanglular paper packages. Made from whole or partly skimmed milk, it's soft, mild and slightly sour with a texture firm enough to slice without crumbling.

10 **ROMANO.** Named for its Roman birthplace, this hard grating cheese is made from partly skimmed milk. It has a yellow-white color and a sharp, piquant flavor that makes it delightful as a seasoning ingredient for other foods.

11 **PARMESAN.** While it is named after the Italian city of Parma, this cheese is today produced in large quantities in the U.S. You can purchase it pre-grated or in pieces. It has a sharp, piquant flavor and is pale yellow in color. Parmesan's hard, granular body is due to long curing—usually from 14 to 20 months. It's nearly always served grated with cooked dishes such as spaghetti, pizza, in or on breads, in salads and soups.

12 **BLUE CHEESE** is the American version of a type of blue-veined cheese whose history dates back to 1070. It was named for the French Bleu, the name given to many Roquefort-type cheeses made throughout France. It's a semisoft, sometimes crumbly cheese made from whole milk, easily recognized by the blue-green mold which marbles or streaks its white interior. Blue has a sharp, piquant, spicy flavor, making it particularly appealing when served with fruits.

13 **STILTON.** This whole milk, semisoft cheese is similar to, but slightly more crumbly than blue cheese. It has a dark, wrinkled melon-like rind and an off-white interior marbled with blue-green mold. Its flavor is piquant, somewhat milder than Gorgonzola. Serve it with biscuits, fruit and dessert.

14 **GORGONZOLA.** While this semisoft cheese is less moist than blue, it is similar in appearance to both blue and Stilton. Its piquant flavor makes Gorgonzola delicious in salads and for dessert with fruit. While it's now made in the U.S., the cheese was first made in 9th century Italy and is named for the village of Gorgonzola, near Milan.

15 **PROVOLONE** is a semi-hard cheese, with a smooth, somewhat plastic body that cuts or slices easily without crumbling. It's yellowish-white in color and mild to piquant or smoky in flavor. Available in either pear-, salami- or spherical-shapes as well as small cuts, provolone often has "rope" marks on its shiny surface, created when the cheese is hung in a sling to age. Perhaps because of its origin, this cheese is popularly thought of for use in Italian cooking. But it is also a favorite snack cheese and is delicious as an appetizer, on sandwiches and for dessert, too.

16 **MOZZARELLA** is a semisoft, creamy-white cheese made from whole or partly skimmed milk. It blends well with a variety of cooked foods because it melts easily and has a delicate flavor. It changes, as it melts, from a stretchy consistency to a chewy one, as anyone who loves pizza knows. Try it for cheeseburgers and in sandwiches, too!

17 **RICOTTA.** This soft, sweet cheese is similar to creamed cottage cheese. Made from whole milk or whole milk and whey, it comes packaged fresh in paper, plastic or metal containers, or dry for grating. When dry, it's usually used as a seasoning; when moist, use it in salads, desserts and cooked food such as lasagna and manicotti. First made in Italy, it is therefore called an Italian cheese. But it is now also made throughout central Europe and in the United States. Ricotta is sometimes called whey cheese when it is made from whole milk and the coagulable material in the whey obtained in the manufacture of cheeses such as Cheddar.

18 **SWISS.** It's the cheese with the "large eyes." The "eyes," or holes, often from ½- to 1-inch in diameter, are gas holes which develop in the curd as the cheese ripens. It is a light yellow, hard-smooth cheese, with a mild, sweetish, nutlike flavor. It was first made in the Emmenthal Valley in Switzerland around 1450 and still goes by the name Emmenthaler in its native land. The first Swiss in this country was made about 1850 by Swiss immigrants and much of it is still being made by their descendants. Often in the U.S., Swiss goes by the name Schweizer or Sweitzer. It is one of the most popular of all our cheeses and is famous for its use in fondues, quiche, in sauces, casseroles, for sandwiches and salads.

19 **JACK CHEESE.** The Jack cheese shown opposite is a more aged version of the Monterey Jack shown on page 8 (see No. 2). We've placed it next to Swiss simply to illustrate how greatly two cheeses, usually identified by their "eyes", can vary. Unlike the Swiss, this Monterey Jack has very small "eyes." Sharp and tangy in flavor, it's a nice compliment to fruit or, grated, as a seasoning ingredient.

20 **MUENSTER OR MUNSTER.** Made from whole milk, Muenster has a semisoft, smooth, waxy body with tiny holes, and is mild to mellow in flavor, somewhere between brick and Limburger. Named for the town of its origin in West Germany, this creamy white cheese with its yellow, tan or white surface, is excellent in salads and on sandwiches.

21 **BRICK.** This is another American original, first made in Wisconsin in the 19th century and thought to be named either for its shape or for the bricks used to press the whey out of the unripened cheese during its manufacture. Brick is made from whole milk and is firm or semisoft with a smooth, waxy body dotted with tiny holes. It is light yellow to orange in color with a caramel-colored rind (this should be removed before eating because of its bitterness). The cheese has a mild to sharp flavor similar to Limburger and some Port Saluts. It's great as a nibbling cheese.

22 **PORT SALUT or PORT DU SALUT** is a semisoft, smooth buttery cheese made from whole and slightly acid milk. Its flavor, depending on aging, can range from mellow to robust, somewhere between Cheddar and Limburger. It has a russet color surface (see adjacent photograph) with a creamy yellow interior dotted by small "eyes" or holes. First made around 1865 by Trappist Monks at the Abbey at Port du Salut in France, its popularity has spread to abbeys in various other parts of Europe, in Canada and in the U.S. It's particularly appropriate as a dessert cheese, served with fresh fruits.

23 **BEL PAESE** means "beautiful country" in Italian, the home of its origin about 1890. Made today in the U.S., Bel Paese-type cheese has a mild, slightly salty flavor and a soft waxy texture that makes it easy to both slice and spread.

24 **BRIE** is a soft, surface-ripened cheese that has a thin, edible crust and a glossy yellow interior, much like the consistency of a thick honey. It is mild to pungent in flavor and as such, is totally compatible with fruits for dessert. Because it spreads easily, Brie is also delightful served on crackers. It was first made several centuries ago in France where it is still produced today, as well as in other European countries and the U.S.

25 **CAMEMBERT** (pronounced Kam-Em-Bear). Legend says that Napoleon named this cheese in 1791 while traveling through the French town of Camembert where he stopped for lunch at a local farmhouse, where the then nameless cheese was made. Having enjoyed the cheese, Napoleon felt it deserved some identity and so named it after the town. So much for fables. But one thing that any cheese lover knows for sure is that this classic dessert cheese has an unforgettable taste and texture. It's mild to pungent, similar but stronger than Bel Paese, with a white to yellow interior that is waxy, creamy or almost fluid, depending on the ripening.

26 **LIEDERKRANZ,** another American original, was first made in Monroe, New York, in 1882. In an attempt to duplicate a favorite German cheese, a cheesemaker named Emil Frey discovered, instead, what turned out to be Liederkranz—which he named after a singing society to which he belonged. Today, this whole milk, surface-ripened cheese is made in the Middle West. It has a soft, creamy texture when fully ripened, and a light, orange-colored soft rind. Made in small, four-ounce loaves, Liederkranz is similar to a mild Limburger in flavor.

SEMISOFT

SOFT

Mozzarella is a semisoft cheese with a smooth, shiny texture and a somewhat stretchy consistency.

Cottage is a soft, uncured, delicate cheese with large or small curds. It comes in either dry or creamed form.

Muenster is a semisoft cheese with a smooth, waxy body and numerous small holes or "eyes."

Blue is a semisoft, crumbly cheese with blue-green veins.

Cream Cheese has a soft, smooth, buttery texture that makes it ideal for spreading.

Port Salut is a semisoft, smooth cheese dotted by small "eyes."

Camembert is a soft cheese with a creamy interior and a thin, edible crust.

BUYING, STORING & SERVING TIPS

IT'S THE ORIGINAL HEALTH FOOD

In its concentrated form, cheese contains almost all the protein, essential minerals, vitamins and other nutrients of milk. And, ounce for ounce, it has the same protein value as meat, fish or poultry. To give you the specifics: 1½ ounces of Cheddar contains about the same calcium as 1 cup of whole, skim or buttermilk; 3 ounces of Cheddar has about the same protein as 3 large eggs, 3 ounces of cooked chicken or beef pot roast. In addition to being nutritious, cheese is also readily digested.

STORING CHEESE PROPERLY

Like all dairy products, cheese is perishable and should, therefore, be kept well wrapped and refrigerated at 35° to 40° to preserve its original flavor and appearance. Here are some pointers:
● Leave cheese in its original wrapper or wrap tightly in wax paper, plastic wrap, plastic bags, foil or in covered containers. Aromatic cheeses (such as Limburger), in particular, should be stored in tightly covered jars or containers, and should be used soon after purchase.
● Unsliced cheese usually keeps longer than sliced cheese because air can't get to it as easily.
● With crumbly cheeses such as blue, smooth the surface with the flat of a knife before wrapping for storage. This will decrease the amount of surface exposed to the air.
● Cheeses should not be kept out of the refrigerator for extended periods. If they are, they may dry out, "oil-off" or become moldy. It's a good idea, therefore, to cut only what you plan to serve or use; and rewrap, and store the remainder.
● If cheese does develop mold, it can still be used. The mold is harmless and can be scraped off—no change in flavor will be noticed unless the mold has penetrated deeply into cracks in the cheese. In such cases, the moldy portion should be discarded. The blue-green veined cheeses are an exception. Their unique flavor comes from the molding process.

A good rule of thumb to remember when storing cheese is that the softer the cheese, the more perishable it is. The following timetable is even more specific.

Cheese	Storage Time
Cottage, Ricotta	Use within 3 to 5 days
Cream, Neufchâtel and other soft cheeses	Use within 2 weeks
Cheddar, Swiss and other hard varieties	Will keep several months*

*Long holding will result in some additional curing (aging) and a sharper flavor.

FREEZING CHEESE

While generally not recommended, you can freeze cheese. The flavor is not affected. However, freezing does damage the body and texture of cheese, causing it to become crumbly and mealy. Therefore, it's suggested that frozen cheese be reserved primarily for cooking purposes, or in salad dressings—where texture doesn't matter.

It's important to store the cheese at 0°F. or lower, properly sealed in either its original package, in freezer wrap or an air-tight container. This will help prevent loss of moisture and subsequent drying. In addition, the cheese should be cut into ½-pound pieces not more than 1 inch thick.

The following cheeses can be frozen up to 6 months: Brick, Camembert, Cheddar, Edam, Gouda, Liederkranz, mozzarella, Muenster, Parmesan, Port du Salut, provolone and Swiss.

The soft cheeses such as cream, cottage and ricotta are not recommended for freezing. They tend to become watery and mealy.

SERVING CHEESE

Cheese has fantastic flexibility, which is obvious when you consider it's one of the few foods that, cooked or uncooked, is welcome at any meal or for any snack or appetizer offering. There's nothing complicated about serving it either, but the following tips are helpful to keep in mind.
● Except for the soft, unripened cheeses such as cottage and cream, cheese should always be served at room temperature. (When it's refrigerator-cold, the flavor is numbed.) To warm the cheese, remove it from the refrigerator anywhere from 30 minutes to an hour ahead of serving time. But leave it in its wrapping while it warms, to prevent drying. Also, certain soft, cured cheeses such as Liederkranz and Camembert, are even more delightful if left out anywhere from one to three hours ahead.
● Before serving the cheese, trim off the cut dried edges of prior servings. If there's any mold around the edges, trim this off, too. It's harmless, but unappealing.
● Do not present bits and pieces of cheese but rather reasonable size portions. Save the small pieces for cooking (see page 18 for ideas on using odds and ends).
● When offering an assortment of cheeses, choose three or more with distinctly different flavors. It's a nice idea to label them, and perhaps mark them mild, medium or sharp.
● A thin bladed knife is best for cutting the hard cheeses.
● For some semisoft cheeses such as blue, use a heavy thread or thin wire for slicing.
● For serving semisoft cheeses such as Camembert or Port du Salut, use a butter knife.

- A cheese scoop (or butter knife) can be used for serving cheeses such as Gouda and Edam. Or, if you prefer, cut them into wedges.
- To allow for easy cutting and serving, do not place crackers on the cheese board, but in a separate dish or basket.

COOKING WITH CHEESE

There are no secrets to cooking with cheese, but there are a few things you should know.

1. Use low heat, just high enough to melt the cheese and blend it with other ingredients. High heat makes the cheese tough and stringy.

2. Avoid long cooking periods. Again, cook cheese just long enough for it to melt. Like high heat, long cooking tends to only make the cheese tough.

3. To avoid long cooking, add cheese as a last ingredient, particularly in sauces, casseroles and toppings. Remember, too, to shred, grate, cube or dice the cheese beforehand so that it melts faster.

4. When broiling foods with cheese toppings, place the broiler pan so that the food is 4 to 5 inches from heat; broil just until the cheese is melted.

5. When baking casseroles with cheese toppings, add the cheese at the end of the baking time (about 5 to 10 minutes), and have the oven between 325° and 375°. Or, cover cheese with crumbs to prevent toughening or hardening while casserole cooks.

6. When preparing fondues, use a heat-proof glass or ceramic saucepan or casserole dish if you don't own a standard earthenware fondue pot.

7. When melting cheese for Welsh Rarebit or other saucy dishes, use a heavy bottomed pan or double-boiler, to prevent scorching of cheese.

CALORIE WATCHING

Since even a small amount of cheese supplies a big nutrition boost, it's an ideal food for calorie watchers. And, for anyone on a bland diet, it offers the bonus of being easy to digest. Certain varieties, such as cottage and farmer cheese, can be enjoyed in full-size portions because their calorie counts are so small. Others, though slightly higher in calories, can also be included on your diet if you use small amounts and follow some of the ideas here.

- Use the sharpest cheese you can find—and use less of it! One tablespoon of shredded extra-sharp Cheddar cheese is worth two tablespoons of mild Cheddar, at half the calories.
- In Italian foods, use grated extra-sharp Romano in place of the milder Parmesan. And, if you like lasagna and ravioli, make it with cottage cheese instead of Italian ricotta. The flavor's similar, but the calories are a lot less—about 175 a cupful, instead of 400.
- Like cheese on your salad? Blue cheese is slight-

ly lower in calories than the similarly flavored Stilton and Gorgonzola. Mix with lumps of mild-flavored, low-fat cottage cheese.

- Grated zippy-sharp Romano mixed with lumps of large-curd cottage cheese can replace the more fattening feta cheese in Greek salads.
- Ounce for ounce, most hard cheeses offer double the protein of luncheon meat . . . so you need only one slice of cheese to equal the value of two slices of lunch meat in a sandwich.
- Here are calorie guidelines for some of the popular natural cheeses: Cheddar, Gouda, Parmesan and Stilton—105 to 120 calories per ounce; blue, cream cheese, Edam, provolone, Muenster and Swiss—95 to 105 calories per ounce; cottage, pot and farmer cheese—20 to 30 calories per ounce.

BUYING TIPS

- Buy cheese at a store that does enough business to suggest that the cheeses do not sit on the shelves beyond their time.
- The cheese should look good. This is a simple rule to remember and it doesn't take an expert eye. If it looks good to you, then it probably is. Here are some specifics on how cheeses should look:

The hard cheeses, such as Cheddar, should not look too dry. While this does not mean the cheese has to be moist-looking, it should, by the same token, not have any cracks on its surface. White mold in the body of the cheese is also an indication the cheese is not fresh.

The veined cheeses, such as blue, Stilton and Gorgonzola, should look moist and the veining or marbling should look appealing. (The veins should contrast with the white or off-white of the body.) If the cheese is too old it will look dry or crumbly.

A semisoft cheese, like any other, should look good to the eye. The natural turnover of cheeses in your supermarket, combined with open dating of some, and the fact that cheeses of the semisoft type keep very well, practically guarantees that freshness will never be a problem. You can buy with ease!

A soft cheese that's packaged so you can't see it (such as Brie), may seem difficult to choose. However, you needn't worry about it being too old or mishandled if you remember the following. The paper or foil packaging should never be broken to expose the cheese; and it should be fresh and clean. If the paper is sticky or has been stained by the cheese, avoid buying. Also, the wrapper should adhere loosely to the cheese; it should not look as if its sinking into the cheese. In addition, a good sniff of the package will tell you a lot. If it smells rank or if it smells at all when it shouldn't depending on the cheese, don't buy it. This tip is one that may take a bit of practice, as learning to become familiar with any cheese does, but the practice will undoubtedly prove most enjoyable.

15

MEASURING UP

Have you ever had to stop in the middle of a recipe to count the tablespoons in a stick of butter? Or spent inordinate time trying to remember how many ounces of cheese to buy when a recipe calls for 1 cup grated? If so, you're in good company, because equivalent measures often escape the most experienced cooks. With this in mind, we offer the following guide. It's a visual primer designed to give instant satisfaction whenever a question of amount occurs. We've also included equivalent measures in all our recipes. For example, instead of listing *4 cups cooked rice* in a recipe, we show it as *4 cups cooked rice (1 cup uncooked)* . . . hopefully a guarantee against disasters! Now, how many ounces did you say are in a pint?

BUTTER MEASUREMENTS

½ stick butter = ¼ cup or 4 tablespoons

1 stick butter = ½ cup or 8 tablespoons

2 sticks butter = 1 cup or ½ pound

4 sticks butter = 2 cups or 1 pound

EVERYDAY & OFT-FORGOTTEN MEASURES

TEASPOONS
1½ teaspoons = ½ tablespoon
3 teaspoons = 1 tablespoon

TABLESPOONS
2 tablespoons = 1 fluid ounce
4 tablespoons = ¼ cup
5 tablespoons plus
1 teaspoon = ⅓ cup
8 tablespoons = ½ cup
10 tablespoons plus
2 teaspoons = ⅔ cup
12 tablespoons = ¾ cup
16 tablespoons = 1 cup

CUPS
1 cup = 8 ounces
2 cups = 16 ounces
4 cups = 32 ounces or
1 quart

PINTS
½ pint = 1 cup
1 pint = 2 cups or
½ quart
2 pints = 4 cups or
1 quart

QUARTS
1 quart = 32 ounces or
4 cups
2 quarts = ½ gallon
4 quarts = 1 gallon

GRATED OR SHREDDED CHEESE MEASUREMENTS

(Note: Also follow these measurements for diced or crumbled cheese.)

¼ cup or 1 ounce ungrated = 4 tablespoons grated cheese

2 ounces ungrated = ½ cup grated cheese

4 ounces or ¼ pound ungrated = 1 cup grated cheese

8 ounces or ½ pound ungrated = 2 cups grated cheese

NOTE: Store-bought grated Parmesan or Romano varies slightly from the measurements above; 1 cup equals 3 ounces instead of the 4 given here. However, all recipes in this book call for measurements by cupfuls, when grated, so you needn't worry about the ounce measurement for Parmesan or Romano. Also: One cup cottage cheese or cream cheese equals 8 ounces; 2 cups = 16 ounces or 1 pound.

1 pound ungrated = 4 cups grated cheese

ODDS & ENDS

There will probably be times when you're left with a tag end of cheese from the appetizer tray, or from a recipe that called for less cheese than you bought. But one of the wonderful things about this food is that it's usable right down to the last shred. Following are some ideas on ways to use up those leftovers. The suggestions are designed to help you economize easily and deliciously.

• Sprinkle leftover shredded Cheddar or provolone over hot chili just before serving.
• Sprinkle shredded Swiss over tomato soup in individual ovenproof soup bowls. Bake in a moderate oven (350°) 10 to 15 minutes, or until the cheese is melted.

ITALIAN HERB STICKS
Halve a loaf of Italian bread lengthwise and crosswise, then split each quarter, as shown here. Brush cut sides with melted butter mixed with any leftover grated cheese you have on hand (Parmesan and Cheddar are good choices). Place on a cooky sheet. Bake in hot oven (425°) five minutes, or until toasty. Place on appetizer tray or in bread basket to serve with dinner.

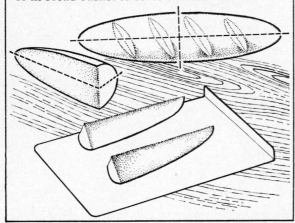

• Sprinkle any leftover cheese into the bottom of lightly buttered muffin cups. Put refrigerated biscuits in each cup and bake according to package directions. Or, if you're making muffins from scratch, sprinkle the cheese right into the batter. Any of the following combinations will be welcome: Cheddar and Swiss; Cheddar and oregano; Cheddar and minced onion; Swiss, provolone and Cheddar; Cheddar and blue.
• Grate any leftover cheese and add to almost any vegetable sauce, or sprinkle on top of vegetables.
• Grate hard or dried up cheese and store in covered jars. Use to sprinkle in or on casseroles, omelets, soups, hot breads, rolls or muffins.

• Prepare packaged Spanish-rice mix and place in a baking dish. Arrange Vienna sausages on top; sprinkle both generously with grated Cheddar. Bake in a hot oven (400°) 20 minutes, or until bubbly hot and cheese melts.
• Bake your favorite frozen peach, apple or cherry pie, following label directions. Serve warm with these extras: On peach pie, a big spoonful of cottage cheese or whipped cream cheese; on apple, a wedge of Camembert; and, on cherry, a spoonful of whipped cream cheese with crushed peanut brittle.
• Blend 2 tablespoons of sour cream and 2 tablespoons of grated Parmesan together in a small bowl. Spread the mixture over leftover slices of cooked, heated chicken. Broil 2 minutes, or until the topping is hot.
• Toss French fried potatoes with grated Parmesan for a nice change-of-pace side dish. For 1 package (9 ounces) of frozen French fries you'll need about 2 ounces of grated Parmesan.
• Beat ½ cup cream-style cottage cheese, ¼ cup crumbled blue, ¼ cup milk and ½ teaspoon of garlic salt until smooth. It becomes a Danish-type dressing that's delicious over lettuce wedges.
• Serve honeydew melon or cantaloupe with wedges of Camembert for a refreshing fruit-and-cheese plate.
• Cut sliced white bread into tiny cubes or pull apart into crumbs, toss with melted butter and grated cheese, and sprinkle over the top of a casserole before baking.
• A little bit of cheese added to a basic white sauce can transform it into a creamy, wonderful topping for meats, vegetables, egg dishes, toast points, or for use as a hot dip for chunks of bread, à la fondue style. Following is a recipe for the white sauce, to which you add ½ cup grated Cheddar (2 ounces).

BASIC WHITE SAUCE

This recipe makes about 1½ cups of sauce.

½ teaspoon grated onion
2 tablespoons butter
2 tablespoons all-purpose flour
¼ teaspoon salt
⅛ teaspoon pepper
1 cup milk

1. Sauté onion in butter 1 minute in a small saucepan; stir in flour, salt and pepper; cook until bubbly. Stir in milk. Continue cooking, stirring constantly, until sauce thickens and boils 1 minute.
2. Stir in the ½ cup grated Cheddar and ½ teaspoon Worcestershire sauce; lower heat, and stir just until cheese is melted. Serve hot. (If using another cheese, follow the same measurements.)

2
THE APPETIZER TRAY

Start with a selection of your favorite cheeses. Add some bread slices, crackers, sausage and, perhaps, a glass of wine. Your no-work appetizer tray is now complete—and it's delicious. On the next 13 pages we offer specific suggestions for these combinations, along with a delightful sampling of other easy-to-do appetizers. They include cheese balls and logs, quick dips, cheese spreads and special-occasion hors d'oeuvres to make ahead. What could be more appetizing?

HAVE A CHEESE AND WINE PARTY

A cheese and wine party is a sociable way to become acquainted with a variety of cheeses and wines, and it has the bonus of being easy to prepare. Here are a few things to keep in mind:
• Select four or five cheeses, ranging from mild to sharp and from creamy smooth to firm in texture. Keep color and shape contrasts in mind, too. Then select an equal number of interesting wines, from mild to robust.
• Allow ½ pound of cheese and ½ bottle of wine for each guest.
• Serve the cheese at room temperature.
• Provide a pitcher of water for rinsing out the wine glasses between tastings, along with a container for the used water.
• Begin the tasting with the mild cheeses and the mellow wines, working your way up to the sharper cheeses and more robust wines.
• Serve cubes of French or Italian bread, crackers and salami with the wine and cheese. The bread and crackers clear the palate.
• Serve appetizer, white, rosé and sparkling wines chilled (about 3 hours in the refrigerator); serve red wines at room temperature.
  The following guide should get you started.

Cheese	Compatible Wines
Blue and Gorgonzola	Claret, burgundy, port, brandy, chianti, champagne
Brie	Port, cognac, calvados
Brick	Rosé, white wine, sherry
Camembert	Port, sherry, madeira, claret, burgundy
Cheddar and Colby	Port, sherry, madeira, claret, burgundy
Cream	Sparkling wines, rosés
Edam	Tokay, cold duck, claret
Gouda	Tokay, cold duck, rosé
Liederkranz and Limburger	Dry red wines
Monterey Jack and Muenster	Rosés, white wines, cream sherry
Neufchâtel	Sparkling wines, rosés, white wines
Port du Salut	Red, white or rosé, light, dry and fruity
Provolone	Dry red, dry white
Stilton	Fruit wines, port, burgundy, cognac, sherry
Swiss	Sauterne, champagne, dry or sweet white wine, sparkling burgundy

Party hors d'oeuvres on page 21 include Pecan Cheese Ball, Italiano-Cream Cheesed Mushrooms, Cheddar-Onion Crackers, Ham-Stuffed Cherry Tomatoes, Blue Cheese-Stuffed Beets and Peruvian Puffs. Recipes are in this chapter.

DIPS & SPREADS

APPETIZER VEGETABLE PLATES
Dunk raw vegetable sinto this creamy dip. It's an easy make-ahead.

Makes 8 servings.

  8 ounces cream cheese, softened
  ½ cup light cream
  1 teaspoon instant minced onion
  ¼ teaspoon salt
  ½ teaspoon Worcestershire sauce
  ¼ cup thinly sliced radishes
  1 tablespoon minced parsley
  4 small tomatoes
    Lettuce
    Zucchini, celery and carrot sticks

1. Beat cream cheese until soft and smooth in a small bowl; beat in cream, onion, salt and Worcestershire sauce; fold in radishes and parsley. Chill.
2. Halve each tomato crosswise. (To flute edge, make even saw-tooth cuts into top of tomato half all the way around.) Scoop out insides of tomatoes with a teaspoon and save to add to a soup; turn tomato cups upside down on paper toweling to drain; chill.
3. When ready to serve, place each tomato cup on a lettuce-lined salad plate; spoon cheese mixture into hollows; garnish with parsley sprigs, if you wish. Frame each with several zucchini, celery and carrot sticks to dip into cheese mixture.

RUSSIAN COTTAGE DIP
With ready-seasoned bottled dressing, you're halfway to a party dip.

Makes about 2¾ cups.

  2 hard-cooked eggs, coarsely chopped
  1 can (2 ounces) anchovy fillets, drained and chopped
  2 cups (16 ounces) cream-style cottage cheese
  ⅓ cup bottled Russian salad dressing

1. Combine chopped eggs and anchovy fillets in a medium-size bowl.
2. Combine cottage cheese and salad dressing in container of electric blender; cover and whirl until smooth. (If you do not have a blender, press cottage cheese through a sieve, then combine thoroughly with the salad dressing.)
3. Stir cheese-salad dressing mixture into egg mixture. Chill several hours to blend flavors. Serve with your favorite crackers or crisp vegetable sticks.

CARAWAY DIP

Here's a nice flavor change for a cream cheese dip.

Makes 1½ cups.

8 ounces cream cheese
3 tablespoons light cream
½ cup finely chopped celery
2 tablespoons caraway seeds
1 teaspoon grated onion
  Few drops liquid red-pepper seasoning

1. Blend cream cheese and cream until smooth in a small bowl.
2. Stir in celery, caraway seeds, onion and red-pepper seasoning. Chill. Serve with crackers or vegetable sticks.

SWEET-SOUR DIP

Sautéed bacon adds a refreshingly crisp touch to this mix-and-serve dip.

Makes about 1⅓ cups.

4 slices bacon
8 ounces cream cheese
¼ cup bottled sweet-sour salad dressing (from an 8-ounce bottle)
2 tablespoons milk

1. Dice bacon slices; sauté until crisp in a small frying pan; remove to paper toweling to drain.
2. Combine cream cheese, sweet-sour dressing and milk in a medium-size bowl; beat until smooth. Fold in bacon.
3. Chill several hours. Serve with crackers or crisp vegetable sticks.

TWIN CHEESE MOLDS

Paper cups are the handy molds for these deviled-ham and sharp-cheese spreads.

Makes 12 servings.

2 cups grated sharp Cheddar cheese (8 ounces)
4 tablespoons (½ stick) butter
1 teaspoon Worcestershire sauce
8 ounces cream cheese
1 can (2¼ or 3 ounces) deviled ham

1. Combine Cheddar cheese, butter and Worcestershire sauce in a medium-size bowl; beat until fluffy. Blend cream cheese and deviled ham until smooth in a second bowl.
2. Pack each mixture into an about-2-cup-size paper cup, smoothing top even. Chill both several hours or overnight.
3. When ready to serve, snip rim of each cup and gently peel off paper; invert cheese molds onto a serving plate. Frame each mold with your favorite assorted crisp crackers, if you wish.

CHEESE CRUNCH

Walnuts add the crunch to this zippy double-cheese dip.

Makes 2½ cups.

2 cups shredded Cheddar cheese (8 ounces)
8 ounces cream cheese, softened
1 teaspoon prepared mustard
¼ cup heavy cream
¼ cup chopped walnuts
2 tablespoons chopped parsley

1. Blend Cheddar cheese, cream cheese, mustard and cream in a medium-size bowl until smooth. Stir in walnuts and parsley. Chill. Take from refrigerator ½ hour before serving to soften. (Beat in a little more cream, if needed, to thin enough for dipping.)
2. Spoon into dip bowls; garnish each with a walnut half, if you wish. Serve with crisp crackers.

TRIPLE CARAWAY SPREAD

Serve this versatile appetizer as a spread, canapé filling—or, roll it into a ball and coat with nuts or bacon bits.

Makes 1½ cups.

3 ounces cream cheese, softened
½ cup (1 stick) butter, at room temperature
½ cup cottage cheese
2 teaspoons anchovy paste
1 teaspoon caraway seed, crushed
1 teaspoon dry mustard
1 teaspoon paprika
1 teaspoon grated onion
  Party-size breads or sandwich bread slices
  Pimiento strips
  Parsley sprigs
  Shrimp, canned
  Cherry tomatoes, halved
  Crushed pecans, bacon bits, chopped parsley or paprika

1. Blend together cream cheese, butter, cottage cheese, anchovy paste, caraway, mustard, paprika and onion in a small-size bowl. Cover; chill several hours, or overnight, to blend flavors.
2. To serve as spread: Remove mixture from refrigerator 30 minutes before serving. Serve at room temperature with party-size breads.
3. To make canapés: Remove crusts from slices of sandwich bread. Spread caraway mixture, softened to room temperature, on bread slices. Garnish with pimiento and parsley sprigs. Cut slices in half and top with shrimp or cherry tomatoes.
4. To make a cheese ball from mixture: Double the recipe above and mix ingredients together, following directions in Step 1. Chill for 1 hour. Then, shape mixture into a ball and roll in chopped pecans, parsley, paprika or bacon bits. Chill in covered container overnight to blend flavors. Serve with a selection of your favorite crackers or party-size breads.

CLAM-CREAM DIP
Your zippy seasoning helper? Versatile horseradish.

Makes 2 cups.

8 ounces cream-style cottage cheese
3 or 4 ounces cream cheese
2 teaspoons prepared horseradish
1 teaspoon Worcestershire sauce
1 can (about 8 ounces) minced clams, drained
3 to 4 tablespoons light cream
   Paprika

1. Blend cottage cheese, cream cheese, horseradish and Worcestershire sauce in a medium-size bowl; stir in clams. Chill.
2. When ready to serve, beat in cream to thin mixture enough for dipping; spoon into small bowls; sprinkle with paprika. Serve with crisp potato chips.

CHICKEN-CHIVE DIP
Meat spread adds special flavor to cottage cheese.

Makes 1⅓ cups.

1 cup (8 ounces) cream-style cottage cheese
1 can (5 ounces) chicken spread
2 tablespoons light cream
1 teaspoon cider vinegar
2 teaspoons finely cut chives

1. Combine cottage cheese, chicken spread, cream and vinegar in a medium-size bowl; beat until smooth. Stir in chives; chill.
2. Spoon into a small bowl; garnish with more cut chives, if you wish, and serve with thin cucumber and carrot "dippers."

CIDER CHEESE SPREAD
This spread keeps well and can be made as many as two or three days ahead. Carve mold into apple shape a day ahead, if you wish, then wrap tightly and chill.

Makes about 3 cups.

8 ounces cream cheese
½ cup apple cider
2 cups shredded Swiss cheese (8 ounces)
2 cups shredded Cheddar cheese (8 ounces)
½ cup (1 stick) butter, melted
   Paprika

1. Beat cream cheese until smooth in a large bowl. Slowly beat in cider, Swiss cheese, Cheddar cheese and melted butter; continue beating until fluffy. Pack into a buttered 3-cup bowl, mounding top. Chill overnight until very firm.
2. Several hours before serving, loosen cheese around edge with a knife; invert onto a cutting board or plate. With a small sharp knife, trim away edge of cheese to round shape like an apple; press a stem from a fresh apple into top. Dust the cheese-apple all over with paprika.
3. Place on a large serving plate. For best flavor, let stand at room temperature at least 30 minutes before serving. Garnish with parsley, if you wish, and serve with party-size rye bread and crisp crackers.

TRIPLE CHEESE MOLD
Mild cream and Cheddar cheeses, plus zesty blue blend in this fluffy spread.

Makes 6 servings.

1 envelope unflavored gelatin
¾ cup water
2 teaspoons Worcestershire sauce
2 teaspoons lemon juice
⅛ teaspoon salt
3 or 4 ounces cream cheese
2 tablespoons crumbled blue cheese
2 tablespoons grated Cheddar cheese
⅓ cup milk
2 tablespoons finely chopped green pepper
½ teaspoon grated onion
½ cup heavy cream

1. Soften gelatin in water in a small saucepan; heat slowly, stirring constantly, just until gelatin dissolves; remove from heat. Stir in Worcestershire sauce, lemon juice and salt. Cool while blending cheese mixture.
2. Blend cream, blue and Cheddar cheeses in a medium-size bowl; beat in milk until smooth. Stir in cooled gelatin mixture, then pepper and onion. Chill 20 minutes, or until as thick as unbeaten egg white.
3. Beat cream until stiff in a small bowl; fold into cheese until no streaks of white remain. Spoon into a 3-cup mold. Chill several hours to firm.
4. Just before serving, run a sharp-tip thin-blade knife around top of mold, then dip mold very quickly in and out of a pan of hot water. Invert onto serving plate; carefully lift off mold.

CREAMY BLUE CHEESE DIP
Fill a bowl with this zesty dip and circle it with crackers, potato chips or raw vegetables.

Makes 2 cups.

8 ounces cream cheese, softened
1 cup (8 ounces) dairy sour cream
1 envelope blue-cheese salad-dressing mix
   Crackers, potato chips
   Carrot or celery sticks, green-pepper slices,
   baby radishes, green onions or cucumber slices

1. Blend cream cheese with sour cream and salad-dressing mix in a small bowl. Chill to blend flavors.
2. Before serving, let dip stand at room temperature about 15 minutes. Serve with crackers, potato chips or raw vegetable sticks and slices.

Opposite: Cheese and fresh fruit are naturally good partners for snacks, or during a tournament between backgammon champs.

CHILI CON QUESO
A popular dunk, to be scooped out with corn chips.

Makes 4 cups.

8 cups Cheddar cheese, diced (2 pounds)
½ cup tomato juice
2 tablespoons onion juice
1 can (4 ounces) green chili peppers, seeded and chopped

Combine cheese, tomato juice, onion juice and green chili peppers in a large saucepan. Cook over low heat, stirring constantly, until cheese is melted and mixture is well blended, about 15 minutes. Serve the dunk hot, with either corn chips or crackers.

DIET DIP APPETIZER
Dip with plenty of snap, served with three raw vegetables. Uncreamed cottage cheese gives it its start.

Makes 6 servings at 83 calories each.

1 can (about 8 ounces) minced clams
1 container (12 ounces) pot cheese
¼ cup skim milk
½ teaspoon onion salt
1 teaspoon Worcestershire sauce
6 ten-inch-long stalks of celery
6 large cauliflowerets
1 large stalk Belgian endive

1. Drain liquid from clams into an electric blender container; add cheese, milk, onion salt and Worcestershire sauce; cover. Beat several minutes, or until smooth; spoon into a medium-size bowl. (If you do not have a blender, beat with electric mixer.
2. Fold clams into cheese; chill at least an hour.
3. Split celery stalks lengthwise; cut each stick into 2-inch lengths. Slice cauliflowerets thin; cut endive lengthwise into sixths.
4. When ready to serve, arrange vegetables in separate piles around edges of 6 salad plates; spoon clam mixture in centers, dividing evenly. Sprinkle clam mixture with paprika, if you wish.
Weight-watcher's serving: ¼ cup clam dip, 12 celery sticks, 1 caulifloweret and ¹/₆ stalk endive.

CHEDDAR-ALE CHEESE SPREAD
Cheese and ale complement each other in this spread.

Makes 2 balls about 4 inches in diameter.

6 cups shredded Cheddar cheese (1½ pounds)
3 ounces cream cheese
4 tablespoons butter, softened
¾ cup ale or beer
1 teaspoon dry mustard
¼ teaspoon crushed red pepper
½ cup finely chopped walnuts
½ cup chopped parsley

1. Beat Cheddar and cream cheese and butter in large bowl with electric mixer until smooth. Gradually beat in ale, mustard and crushed red pepper. If mixture is very soft, refrigerate until firm enough to hold its shape.
2. Divide mixture in half and shape into 2 balls. Place on serving plates or boards. Cover with a cheese cover or plastic film. Refrigerate. Keeps well for several weeks.
3. Just before serving, combine walnuts and parsley on a sheet of wax paper and roll cheese balls in mixture to cover completely.

CHEESE BALLS

PECAN CHEESE BALL
This is one of those make-ahead appetizers that belongs in every cook's recipe file.

Makes 1 cheese ball, about 5½ inches in diameter.

4 ounces blue cheese, softened
1 pound (16 ounces) cream cheese, softened
2 cups grated sharp Cheddar cheese (8 ounces)
1 tablespoon grated onion
½ cup chopped pecans
   Parsley

1. Soften cheeses at room temperature. Combine the cheeses with onion until well blended.
2. Line a 1½-pint mixing bowl with plastic wrap. Turn cheese mixture into bowl, packing it down firmly. Refrigerate 1 hour.
3. Turn cheese ball out onto serving platter. Remove plastic wrap. Sprinkle with pecans; decorate with parsley, as shown in the photograph on pages 20-21.

PECAN CREAM BALLS
They double perfectly as dressing and garnish for an appetizer fruit cup or salad.

Makes 4 dozen.

1 cup (8 ounces) uncreamed cottage cheese
1 tablespoon dairy sour cream
1 tablespoon sugar
½ teaspoon grated lemon rind
¼ teaspoon lemon juice
¼ teaspoon vanilla
¼ cup chopped pecans
¼ cup flaked coconut

1. Blend cottage cheese with sour cream, sugar, lemon rind and juice, and vanilla in a medium-size bowl; chill several hours, or until firm.

2. Mix pecans and coconut in a large, shallow bowl.
3. Roll cottage-cheese mixture, a teaspoonful at a time, into a ball, then roll in pecan mixture. Place in a shallow pan; chill again.

TRIPLE-CHEESE BALL
Three kinds of cheese are used to make this extra good appetizer ball.

Makes 16 servings.

1½ pounds cream-style cottage cheese (3 cups)
1½ pounds (24 ounces) cream cheese, softened
1½ cups crumbled blue cheese (6 ounces)
 1 teaspoon seasoned salt
 2 teaspoons Worcestershire sauce
   Few drops red-pepper seasoning
¾ cup finely chopped parsley
 4 large carrots, pared and sliced diagonally
 2 large cucumbers, scored and sliced
 8 stalks celery, sliced
 2 large green peppers, quartered, seeded and cut in bite-size pieces
 1 small head of cauliflower, separated in flowerets
   Corn snacks

1. Combine cottage, cream and blue cheeses, seasoned salt, Worcestershire sauce and red-pepper seasoning in a large bowl; beat until completely blended; cover. Chill several hours, or until firm enough to handle.
2. Spoon cheese mixture in the center of a large serving tray; pat into a mound, then press parsley into cheese to cover.
3. Arrange carrot, cucumber and celery slices, green-pepper pieces, cauliflowerets and corn snacks in separate piles around cheese.

PECAN-CHEESE LOG
Stripes of pecans add a pretty trim and pleasing crunch to this appetizer.

Makes 12 servings.

 8 ounces cream cheese, softened
 1 cup grated Swiss cheese (4 ounces)
 1 cup crumbled blue cheese (4 ounces)
½ teaspoon liquid red-pepper seasoning
¼ cup chopped pecans

1. Blend cream cheese, Swiss cheese, blue cheese and red-pepper seasoning in a medium-size bowl. Chill until firm enough to handle.
2. Shape into an 8-inch-long log; wrap in wax paper, foil or transparent wrap and chill again until firm.
3. To make spiral trim, unwrap log; press ½-inch-wide strips of foil or wax paper diagonally, 1 inch apart, over top and side. Roll log in chopped pecans; chill again.
4. When ready to serve, carefully peel off paper; place log on a serving plate. Frame with crackers.

WALNUT-CHEDDAR LOG
Keep one of these in the refrigerator and you're ready for any last-minute guests.

Makes 12 servings.

 2 cups grated sharp Cheddar cheese (8 ounces)
 4 tablespoons (½ stick) butter
½ teaspoon Worcestershire sauce
½ cup finely chopped walnuts

1. Combine the Cheddar cheese, butter and Worcestershire sauce in a medium-size bowl; beat until well blended and fluffy.
2. Shape cheese mixture into a 6-inch-long log; roll in chopped walnuts. Wrap in wax paper, foil or transparent wrap; chill.

CHEDDAR BALLS
Each little puff—so rich with cheese—just melts in your mouth.

Bake at 400° for 12 minutes. Makes 4 dozen.

½ cup (1 stick) butter
 1 cup grated sharp Cheddar cheese (4 ounces)
1¼ cups sifted all-purpose flour
¼ teaspoon salt
¼ teaspoon paprika

1. Cream butter with cheese until smooth in a medium-size bowl. Blend in flour, salt and paprika, then knead lightly with hands to form a soft dough.
2. Roll, about a teaspoonful at a time, into marble-size balls between palms of hands; place on greased cooky sheets.
3. Bake in hot oven (400°) 12 minutes, or until firm and golden. Serve warm.

TO MAKE SPIRAL TRIM FOR PECAN-CHEESE LOG
Shape the cheese mixture into an 8-inch long log, as directed in recipe at left. Wrap the log and chill until firm. When firm, press ½-inch-wide strips of foil or wax paper diagonally, one inch apart, around log. Roll in chopped nuts. Chill again; peel off foil. Another time, use sesame seeds in place of the nuts.

COLD APPETIZERS

BLUE CHEESE STUFFED BEETS
These zesty vegetable-cheese bites are a beautiful addition to the appetizer or salad plate.

Makes about 2 dozen.

 2 ounces blue cheese, softened
 3 ounces cream cheese, softened
 1 teaspoon Worcestershire sauce
 1 tablespoon chopped chives
 2 cans (1 pound each) small whole beets, drained

1. Combine blue cheese, cream cheese, Worcestershire sauce and chives until well blended.
2. Hollow out beets, using either the point of a paring knife or a small melon scoop. Spoon cheese mixture into hollowed beets. Chill thoroughly.

CHEDDAR-ONION CRACKERS
Served hot or cold, these tangy little morsels will disappear before you know it.

Bake at 375° for 5 minutes. Makes 24 bite-size snacks.

24 small slices sharp Cheddar cheese (from a 10-ounce bar)
24 square whole wheat crackers
 3 medium-size yellow onions, thinly sliced
24 slices pimiento-stuffed olives

1. Arrange a cheese slice on each cracker. Top with an onion ring and olive slice.
2. Bake in a moderate oven (375°) about 5 minutes, or just until the cheese melts slightly. Serve hot. Or, serve cold, without any baking.

HAM CRISPS
Each is just two bites of a cracker stacked with cucumber and spicy deviled ham.

Makes 2½ dozen.

 8 ounces cream cheese
 1 can (4½ ounces) deviled ham
 ¼ cup mayonnaise or salad dressing
 2 teaspoons prepared mustard
 ⅛ teaspoon salt
   Dash of pepper
 2 tablespoons sweet-pickle relish
30 small round crackers
 1 small cucumber, sliced thin
   Parsley

1. Soften cream cheese in a small bowl; beat in deviled ham, mayonnaise or salad dressing, mustard, salt, pepper and pickle relish. Chill several hours.
2. Just before serving, spread about ½ teaspoonful ham mixture on each cracker; top each with a cucumber slice, then a heaping teaspoonful ham mixture. Garnish each with parsley.

PARTY CANAPÉS
Fix these fancies ahead and freeze, ready for a party or drop-in guests.

Makes 2 dozen.

 4 tablespoons butter, softened
 3 or 4 ounces cream cheese
 ½ teaspoon Worcestershire sauce
 2 hard-cooked eggs, shelled
 3 slices white bread
 3 slices whole-wheat bread

1. Blend butter, cream cheese and Worcestershire sauce until smooth in a medium-size bowl; spoon half into a second bowl.
2. Halve eggs; remove yolks; press through a sieve and blend into mixture in one bowl. Cover bowl and set aside with whites for decorating canapés.
3. Trim crusts from bread; cut out 12 rounds with a 1½-inch cutter from 3 slices; cut 12 diamond shapes from remaining slices. Spread each with plain cheese mixture. Decorate and freeze, following directions in Steps 4–6.
4. To decorate: Fill a cake-decorating set with cream-cheese-egg mixture; fit with star tip; pipe an edging around each canapé.
5. Garnish each with small whole shrimps, slivers of smoked salmon rolled up, bits of king crab meat or lobster, sliced stuffed green or ripe olives, capers, cut-up gherkins, diced pimiento, small pickled onions or diced hard-cooked egg white.
6. To freeze: Place canapés in a single layer in a large shallow pan; cover tightly with transparent wrap; freeze. When frozen, pack in boxes no more than two layers deep with transparent wrap between, until ready to use.
7. To thaw: Remove canapés from freezer 1 hour before serving; place in a single layer; let stand at room temperature. Plan to use frozen canapés within two weeks.

STUFFED CELERY
Zippy cheese spread fills bite-size pieces of celery for this crunchy appetizer.

Makes 8 servings.

 3 or 4 ounces cream cheese, softened
 ½ teaspoon Worcestershire sauce
 ½ teaspoon lemon juice
 1 tablespoon finely chopped pistachio nuts
 8 three-inch-long pieces of celery

1. Blend cream cheese, Worcestershire sauce and lemon juice until smooth in a small bowl; stir in pistachio nuts.
2. Spread about 1 tablespoon cheese mixture into hollow in each piece of celery.

ITALIANO-CREAM CHEESE MUSHROOMS
A make-ahead appetizer that requires no cooking.

Makes 12 filled mushrooms.

12 large fresh mushrooms (about 2 inches in diameter)
8 ounces cream cheese, softened
1 package (.6 ounces) Italian-style salad dressing mix
Ripe olive slices

1. Carefully remove stems from mushrooms (reserve for another use). Carefully wipe clean with a damp cloth or towel.
2. Combine softened cream cheese and salad dressing mix until thoroughly blended.
3. Fill mushroom caps with cream cheese mixture, using 2 teaspoons or a pastry bag fitted with a star tip. Garnish each mushroom with 2 ripe olive slices, as shown in photograph on page 21. Chill thoroughly.

PÂTÉ MINIATURES
Zippy pâté, molded in tiny muffin cups, just fits atop store-bought toast rounds.

Makes 24 melba-toast rounds.

1 envelope unflavored gelatin
1 can condensed beef consomme
3 tablespoons water
4 pitted ripe olives, sliced
1 can (4½ ounces) liver pâté
1 can (4½ ounces) deviled ham
4 ounces cream cheese
½ teaspoon grated onion
24 melba-toast rounds

1. Soften gelatin in consomme in a small saucepan; heat just until gelatin dissolves; remove from heat; stir in water.
2. Place an olive slice in each of 24 tiny muffin-pan cups. Spoon 1 teaspoon gelatin mixture into each; chill 10 minutes, or until sticky-firm.
3. Blend liver pâté with deviled ham, cream cheese, grated onion and ¼ cup of the gelatin mixture in a small bowl; spoon 1 tablespoon over sticky-firm layer in each cup. Chill again until sticky-firm.
4. Spoon remaining gelatin mixture over each, dividing evenly; chill several hours, or until firm.
5. Just before serving, loosen each mold around edge with a knife, then dip pan *very quickly* in and out of hot water. Cover with a large flat plate or cooky sheet; turn upside down; lift off pan. Place each mold on a melba-toast round.

HAM-STUFFED CHERRY TOMATOES
One-bite tomatoes, stuffed with a tangy filling, are a colorful addition to your hors d'oeuvres tray.

Makes 36 stuffed tomatoes.

½ cup very finely chopped cooked ham
¼ cup crumbled blue cheese (1 ounce)
¼ cup dairy sour cream
¼ teaspoon lemon juice
Dash of pepper
36 cherry tomatoes
Sprigs of parsley

1. Combine ham, cheese, sour cream, lemon juice and pepper in a small bowl; blend well. Refrigerate until ready to use.
2. With a sharp small knife, cut the tops of the tomatoes and scoop out the insides. Spoon about ½ teaspoon of ham-and-cheese mixture into each tomato, mounding slightly. Garnish each tomato with a small sprig of parsley.
3. Party day: Prepare in morning. Refrigerate until ready to use.

PIZZA POPCORN
Big kernels of corn are tossed with seasoned butter.

Makes 8 cups.

4 tablespoons (½ stick) butter
1 clove garlic, minced
¼ teaspoon leaf oregano, crumbled
¼ teaspoon leaf basil, crumbled
8 cups freshly popped corn
½ teaspoon onion salt
2 tablespoons grated Parmesan cheese

1. Melt butter in a small saucepan; stir in garlic, oregano and basil. Heat 1 to 2 minutes.
2. Pour over popcorn in a large bowl; sprinkle with onion salt and cheese; toss lightly until coated.

FARMHOUSE CHEESE RELISH
This lazy-day recipe is a good choice for an old-fashioned relish tray.

Makes 4 servings.

1 cup (8 ounces) cream-style cottage cheese
1 medium-size dill pickle, diced and drained (¼ cup)
1 small carrot, shredded (¼ cup)
2 tablespoons dairy sour cream
2 tablespoons mayonnaise or salad dressing

1. Combine cottage cheese, dill pickle and carrots in a medium-size bowl. Fold in sour cream and mayonnaise or salad dressing until well blended.
2. Chill until serving time. Sprinkle lightly with paprika, if you wish.

DOUBLE CHEESE CHIPS
Cream and blue cheeses, molded and cut into tiny squares, top crisp crackers.

Makes 4 dozen.

- 1 envelope unflavored gelatin
- 1 envelope instant chicken broth
- 1 cup milk
- 3 or 4 ounces cream cheese
- ¼ cup crumbled blue cheese (1 ounce)
- 48 small snack crackers (from a 9-ounce box)
  Dairy sour cream
  Pickled sweet red pepper, seeded and cut
  into tiny cubes

1. Mix gelatin, instant chicken broth and milk in a small saucepan; heat slowly, stirring constantly, just until gelatin dissolves; remove from heat.
2. Beat in cream cheese and blue cheese; pour into a baking pan, 8x8x2. (Layer will be a scant ½-inch thick.) Chill several hours, or until firm.
3. Cut out 48 tiny squares from molded cheese. Make each appetizer with a cracker, dab of sour cream, cheese square and red-pepper garnish.
Note: Canapés can be put together about an hour ahead, then chilled until serving time.

HOT APPETIZERS

MINIATURE WIENER WELLINGTONS
Stuffed cocktail frankfurters are wrapped in dough.

Bake at 375° for 10 minutes. Makes 16 servings.

- ¼ pound piece liverwurst or Braunschweiger
- 2 tablespoons grated Parmesan cheese
- ½ teaspoon onion salt
- 2 packages (8 ounces each) cocktail frankfurters
- 2 packages refrigerated crescent dinner rolls

1. Peel casing from liverwurst; slice meat into 8 rounds. Cut each round into 4 strips; trim strips, if needed, to fit into cocktail frankfurters.
2. Mix cheese and onion salt on wax paper; roll each strip of liverwurst in cheese mixture.
3. Split each frankfurter almost to bottom; stuff with a strip of seasoned liverwurst; cut each in half.
4. Unroll crescent dough, one package at a time, into 2 rectangles; pinch together at perforations. Cut each rectangle crosswise into 16 one-inch-wide strips; wrap each around a half frankfurter. Repeat with remaining package of rolls. Place rolls, seam side down, on a cooky sheet.
5. Bake in moderate oven (375°) 10 minutes, or until golden. Serve while still hot.

SAUSAGE TARTLETS
Tiny tarts with a savory filling.

Bake shells at 400° for 5 minutes, then at 375° for 15 minutes. If made ahead, reheat at 400° for 10 minutes. Makes about 5 dozen.

- 1 package piecrust mix
- 5 brown 'n serve sausages (½ an 8-ounce package)
- ¼ pound mushrooms, finely chopped
- 1 small onion, chopped (¼ cup)
- 1 egg
- ½ cup milk
- ½ cup shredded Cheddar cheese (2 ounces)
- ½ teaspoon salt
- ½ teaspoon leaf marjoram, crumbled
- ¼ teaspoon pepper

1. Prepare piecrust mix, following label directions. Pinch off small pieces; press into 1¼-inch tartlet pans. If tartlet pans are not available, tiny muffin pans may be used, pressing the piecrust mix about half way up the sides of the cups. Place tartlet pans in a jelly-roll pan for ease in handling.
2. Bake in hot oven (400°) 5 minutes. Remove to wire rack.
3. Cut sausages into very thin slices. Brown in a small skillet; remove to paper toweling with a slotted spoon. Sauté mushrooms and onion in pan drippings until just tender.
4. Beat egg slightly in a medium-size bowl; add milk, cheese, salt, marjoram and pepper. Mix well. Fill tartlet shells, dividing sausage slices evenly.
5. Bake in moderate oven (375°) 15 minutes, or until firm. Remove to wire rack. Let stand a few minutes before removing tartlets from pans.
6. Do-ahead note: Place tartlets in foil or plastic boxes; cover firmly; label and freeze.
7. Party day: Place tartlets in jelly-roll pan. Heat in hot oven (400°) about 10 minutes, or until piping-hot. Garnish each with a thin slice of stuffed olive, if you wish. Keep hot on hot tray.

SESAME SALMON TURNOVERS
Ready-made dough and a peppy salmon filling are quickly put together.

Bake at 400° for 10 minutes. If made ahead, reheat at 425° for 5 minutes. Makes 8 dozen.

- 1 can (3¾ ounces) salmon, drained, boned and flaked
- 3 ounces cream cheese, softened
- 1 teaspoon mayonnaise or salad dressing
- 1 egg, separated
- 1 tablespoon chopped stuffed olives
- ½ teaspoon dried dill weed
- 1 teaspoon instant minced onion
  Dash liquid red-pepper seasoning
- 3 packages refrigerated crescent dinner rolls
- ¼ cup sesame seeds

1. Combine salmon, cream cheese, mayonnaise or salad dressing, egg yolk, olives, dill weed, onion and pepper seasoning in a small bowl; blend well.
2. Unroll refrigerated rolls, ½ package at a time. Roll the dough in one piece to a 15x6-inch rectangle on a lightly floured pastry board. Cut into circles with a 2-inch cooky cutter (16 circles from each ½ package). Place ¼ teaspoon of filling in center of each round; brush the edges with a little of the egg white; fold dough over filling; press edges together; seal by crimping with tines of a fork. Place, 1 inch apart, on large cooky sheets. Brush tops with remaining egg white; sprinkle with sesame seeds.
3. Bake in hot oven (400°) 10 minutes, or until the turnovers are golden.
4. Do-ahead note: Place turnovers in foil or plastic boxes; cover firmly; label and freeze.
5. Party day: Place on cooky sheets. Heat in hot oven (425°) 5 minutes, or until piping-hot. Keep the turnovers hot on an electric hot tray.

SPINACH-CHEESE PUFFS

These multilayered pastries filled with spinach and cheese can be made and refrigerated ahead of time, then baked just before serving. The secret to their triangular shape—just fold like a flag.

Bake at 375° for 20 minutes. Makes about 44 appetizers.

    2 eggs
    1 medium-size onion, quartered
    2 cups feta cheese, crumbled (8 ounces)
    8 ounces cream cheese, softened
    1 package (10 ounces) frozen chopped spinach, thawed
    2 tablespoons chopped parsley
    1 tablespoon chopped fresh dill or 1 teaspoon dill weed
      Dash pepper
    2 packages (2 ounces each) phyllo or strudel leaves
    1 cup (2 sticks) butter, melted

1. Combine eggs, onion and feta cheese in container of electric blender. Whirl at medium speed, until smooth; add cream cheese; whirl again a few seconds until smooth. Squeeze spinach with hands to remove as much liquid as possible. Add to cheese mixture with parsley, dill and pepper; blend just until combined. Refrigerate at least 1 hour.
2. Stack 2 leaves (16x22 inches each) of phyllo pastry on working surface; cover with plastic wrap to prevent drying. For each puff cut off a strip 2 inches wide and 16 inches long, cutting through both leaves; brush with melted butter.
3. Place a rounded teaspoon filling on one end of strip. Fold one corner to opposite side, forming a triangle. Continue folding, keeping triangle shape, to other end. Arrange the filled pastries on an ungreased jelly-roll pan. Repeat with remaining pastry and filling until all is used.

4. Bake in moderate oven (375°) 20 minutes, or until golden brown. Serve hot.
Note: If you wish, pastries may be filled and shaped, then wrapped and frozen in a single layer until ready to serve. Bake frozen pastries as directed above.

CRAB CROUSTADES
Tiny squares of bread hold nibbles of crab meat.

Bake at 400° for 10 minutes. If made ahead, reheat at 400° for 10 minutes. Makes about 4 dozen.

    1 loaf unsliced white bread
    ½ cup (1 stick) butter, melted
    1¼ cups shredded Cheddar Cheese (5 ounces)
    1 egg yolk
    1 can (7½ ounces) crab meat, drained and flaked
    1 teaspoon Worcestershire sauce
    ¼ teaspoon onion powder
    ⅛ teaspoon pepper

1. Cut bread into 1-inch slices; remove crusts. Cut trimmed slices into 1-inch cubes. Hollow out each cube with a small sharp knife, leaving a shell about ⅛ inch thick; brush sides and tops with melted butter. Place on cooky sheets.
2. Bake in hot oven (400°) 10 minutes, or until crisp and brown. Remove to wire racks; cool.
3. Blend cheese with egg yolk. Add crab meat, Worcestershire, onion powder and pepper; mix.
4. Fill croustades with crab meat mixture.
5. Do-ahead note: Place filled croustades in foil or plastic boxes; cover firmly; label and freeze.
6. Party day: Remove croustades from freezer; place on cooky sheet. Heat in hot oven (400°) 10 minutes, or until filling just starts to brown. Garnish with paprika and parsley. Keep hot on hot tray.

PERUVIAN PUFFS
This savory filling may be made hours ahead. Use a pastry bag and tube for easy handling.

Makes 30 puffs.

    ½ cup grated Parmesan cheese (2 ounces)
    ½ cup mayonnaise or salad dressing
    1½ teaspoons anchovy paste
    1 teaspoon minced onion
    1 container (3¼ ounces) cocktail-size pastry shells (croutelettes)—(about 30)
    1 jar (2¾ ounces) tiny cocktail shrimp
      Parsley

1. Combine the Parmesan cheese, mayonnaise, anchovy paste and onion in a small bowl.
2. Spoon mixture evenly into cocktail-size pastry shells. Place on jelly-roll pan.
3. Run under broiler until tops are bubbly and beginning to brown, about 1 minute. Garnish with cocktail shrimp and parsley, if you wish. Serve hot.

ALSATIAN CHEESE TARTS
Similar to a French fancy, these little gems have a mellow Cheddar-bacon filling.

Bake at 400° for 3 minutes, then at 325° for 25 minutes. Makes 8 tarts.

    2 cups sifted all-purpose flour
 ½ teaspoon salt
 ⅔ cup shortening
    4 to 5 tablespoons cold water
 12 slices bacon
    1 cup grated Cheddar cheese (4 ounces)
 ¾ cup milk
    2 tablespoons butter
      Dash of cayenne
    3 eggs
    2 teaspoons grated onion

1. Sift flour and salt into a medium-size bowl; cut in shortening with a pastry blender until mixture is crumbly. Sprinkle water over top, 1 tablespoon at a time; mix lightly with a fork until pastry holds together and leaves side of bowl clean.
2. Roll out, half at a time, to a 10-inch square on a lightly floured pastry cloth or board; cut out 4 five-inch rounds. (A saucer makes a good pattern.) Fit rounds into 3-inch tart-shell pans. Repeat with second half of pastry to make 8 shells in all. Set pans in a large shallow pan for easy handling.
3. Bake in hot oven (400°) 3 minutes; remove from oven. Lower heat to slow (325°).
4. Dice 4 slices of the bacon; sauté until crisp in a frying pan; remove and drain on paper toweling. Sprinkle bacon and cheese evenly into tart shells.
5. Combine milk, butter and cayenne in a small saucepan; heat slowly until butter melts. Beat eggs slightly in a small bowl; stir in milk mixture slowly, then grated onion. Pour over bacon and cheese.
6. Bake in slow oven (325°) 25 minutes, or just until custard sets; remove from oven. Cool on a wire rack about 2 minutes; loosen around edges with a knife. Remove from pans; place on a serving plate.
7. While tarts bake, sauté remaining bacon until almost crisp in same frying pan, then before removing from pan, roll each slice around the tines of a fork to make a curl; drain on paper toweling. Place on top of tarts; garnish with parsley. Serve hot.

BAKED CLAMS
Each little shell holds a savory stuffing of clams, cheese and parsley.

Bake at 375° for 15 minutes. Makes 8 servings.

    1 can (about 8 ounces) minced clams, drained
 1½ cups soft bread crumbs (3 slices)
 ¼ cup grated Cheddar cheese (1 ounce)
    1 tablespoon chopped parsley
 ¼ teaspoon garlic salt
    2 tablespoons olive or salad oil
 ½ teaspoon lemon juice

1. Combine all ingredients in a small bowl; toss lightly to mix; spoon into 8 scrubbed clam shells or small foil muffin-pan cups. Place shells or cups on a cooky sheet for easy handling. Chill if made ahead.
2. Just before serving, bake in moderate oven (375°) 15 minutes, or until golden. Arrange on platter.

BLUE CHEESE BURGER BALLS
Rolled in crumbs or wrapped in bacon, these appetizers will please the most demanding palates.

Makes 20 appetizers.

 ½ pound ground beef
    1 egg, beaten
 ½ cup crumbled blue cheese
 ½ cup soft bread crumbs
 ½ teaspoon salt
      Dry bread crumbs
 10 slices bacon, halved (optional)

1. Mix beef, egg, cheese, ½ cup bread crumbs and salt in a medium-size bowl. Shape into 20 appetizer-size balls (each about 1-inch in diameter).
2. Roll balls in bread crumbs until well coated, or wrap 1 piece of bacon around each, fastening with wet wooden pick. Place the appetizer balls on baking pan with a wire rack.
3. If crumb-coated, bake the balls in hot oven (400°) 15 minutes. If wrapped with bacon, broil balls 10 minutes, turning occasionally to brown bacon on all sides. Serve hot.

BITSY BURGERS
One of America's favorite snacks is offered here on a miniature scale.

Bake at 375° for 14 minutes. Makes 40 patties.

    1 pound ground beef
    1 teaspoon seasoned salt
    5 slices Cheddar cheese
    4 tablespoons (½ stick) butter
    2 tablespoons prepared mustard
    5 split hamburger buns
 10 cherry tomatoes, sliced thin
    8 small white onions, peeled and sliced thin

1. Mix ground beef and seasoned salt lightly in a small bowl; shape into 40 one-inch patties. Place in a single layer in a shallow baking pan.
2. Bake in moderate oven (375°) for 10 minutes.
3. Cut each cheese slice into 9 squares; place one over each meat patty. Bake 4 minutes longer, or until cheese melts slightly.
4. While meat cooks, blend butter and mustard in a cup. Toast hamburger buns in oven; spread with butter mixture; cut each half in 4 triangles.
5. When ready to serve, place each meat patty on a bun triangle; top with a slice each of tomato and onion; hold in place with a wooden pick. Serve hot.

3
BREADS & SANDWICHES

Hot or cold, dainty or Dagwood-size, what could be more popular than a cheese sandwich? A loaf of cheese bread, perhaps! Here we offer a selection of both, beginning with breads, muffins and bread-sticks. Then there are open-face and tea sandwiches to try, lunch-and-dinner sandwiches and those perennial favorites, cheeseburgers and pizza. They're recipes that transform a traditional idea into a mouth-watering experience—with a pinch of imagination and a slice of cheese, please!

BREADS & BREAD STICKS

PARMESAN GARLIC BREAD
Brush pans with garlic butter to give just a tease of garlic flavor to bread.

Bake at 400° for 40 minutes for large loaves, 30 to 35 minutes for small. Makes two 2-pound loaves or 8 medium-size loaves or 14 miniature loaves.

- 2 cups milk
- 2 tablespoons sugar
- 2 teaspoons salt
- 2 packages active dry yeast
- 2 cups very warm water
- 10 cups sifted all-purpose flour
- 1 cup grated Parmesan cheese
- 2 tablespoons butter, melted
- 1 clove garlic, crushed
  Grated Parmesan cheese

1. Heat milk with sugar and salt in small saucepan just to lukewarm.
2. Sprinkle yeast into very warm water in a large bowl. ("Very warm" water should feel comfortably warm when dropped on wrist.) Stir until yeast dissolves, then stir in cooled milk mixture.
3. Beat in 5 cups flour and 1 cup cheese until completely blended. Beat in remaining flour gradually to make a soft dough.
4. Turn out onto lightly floured pastry board; knead until smooth and elastic, adding only enough extra flour to keep dough from sticking.
5. Place in greased large bowl; turn to coat all over with shortening; cover with a clean towel. Let rise in warm place, away from draft, 1 hour, or until double in bulk. Stir garlic into butter. Brush pans or casseroles with garlic butter.
6. Punch dough down; knead 1 minute on lightly floured pastry board, then shape this way: For large loaves, divide dough in half, divide each half in 7 even pieces, shape into rolls; place 6 rolls around edge of prepared pan and 1 in center. For medium-size loaves: Divide dough into 16 even pieces; shape into rolls, place 2 rolls in each of 8 prepared ten-ounce casserole or custard cups. For miniature loaves: Divide dough into 14 pieces, shape into loaves, place in prepared toy-size loaf pans; cover. Let rise again in warm place, away from draft, 45 minutes, or until double in bulk. Brush tops with water, sprinkle with extra cheese.
7. Bake in very hot oven (400°) 40 minutes for large loaves, 30 to 40 minutes for small and medium loaves, or until breads give a hollow sound when tapped. Remove from pans to wire racks; cool.

EASY CHEESE BOREKS
These feathery, Turkish cheese-filled pastries are perfect to round out a soup and salad supper. Made the long-winded way, they take hours.

Bake at 375° for 15 minutes. Makes 16 boreks.

- 6 ounces cream cheese with chives, softened to room temperature
- 2 tablespoons grated Parmesan cheese
- 1 teaspoon Worchestershire sauce
- 2 to 3 drops liquid red-pepper seasoning
- 2 packages (8 ounces each) refrigerated crescent dinner rolls

1. Blend together cream cheese, Parmesan, Worcestershire and pepper-seasoning; reserve.
2. Unroll crescent rolls—do not separate at the perforations—then pat each of the 8 pieces to form a 4x6-inch rectangle. Cut each piece in half to form 2 squares. Spread 2 teaspoons of the cheese mixture over each piece of dough; roll, jelly-roll fashion.
3. Place boreks seam side down on an ungreased cooky sheet. Seal ends by crimping firmly with the tines of a fork. Bake, uncovered, in a moderate oven (375°), for about 15 minutes, or until the boreks are lightly browned.

CHEDDAR CHEESE BREAD
Each slice of this mellow moist bread has a snappy Cheddar taste.

Bake at 350° for 45 minutes for medium-size loaves, 30 minutes for miniature ones. Makes 4 medium-size loaves, or 2 medium-size and 6 miniature loaves, or 12 miniature loaves.

- 1 cup milk
- 2 tablespoons sugar
- 3 teaspoons salt
- 1 tablespoon butter
- 1 package active dry yeast or 1 cake compressed yeast
- 1 cup very warm water
- 5 cups sifted all-purpose flour
- 2 cups grated sharp Cheddar cheese (8 ounces)

1. Scald milk with sugar, salt and butter in a small saucepan; cool to lukewarm.
2. Sprinkle or crumble yeast into very warm water in a large bowl. ("Very warm" water should feel comfortably warm when dropped on wrist.) Stir until yeast dissolves, then stir in cooled milk.
3. Beat in 1 cup of the flour; sprinkle cheese over and beat in until completely blended. Beat in remaining flour gradually to make a stiff dough.
4. Turn out onto a lightly floured pastry cloth or board; knead until smooth and elastic, adding only enough extra flour to keep dough from sticking to pastry cloth or board.
5. Place in a greased bowl; turn to coat all over with shortening; cover with a clean towel. Let

rise in warm place, away from draft, 1 hour, or until double in bulk.

6. Punch dough down; knead a few times, then shape this way: If making all medium-size loaves, divide dough in quarters; shape each into a loaf. If making medium-size and miniature loaves, divide dough in half; shape one half into 2 loaves, then divide remaining half into sixths; shape each into a loaf. If making all miniature loaves, divide all the dough in twelfths; shape each into a loaf. Place medium-size loaves in greased pans, 7½x3¾x2¼; miniature ones in greased toy-size loaf pans; cover. Let rise again in warm place, away from draft, about 1 hour, or until double.

7. Bake in moderate oven (350°) 45 minutes for medium-size loaves, 30 minutes for miniature ones, or until bread gives a hollow sound when tapped. Remove from pans; brush tops with more butter; cool on wire racks.

Wrapping tip: Cool bread completely, then wrap in transparent wrap.

CHEDDAR CHEESE TWISTS
Start with refrigerated dinner rolls and you'll have these made in nothing flat. (Shown on pages 52–53.)

Bake at 375° for 12 minutes. Makes 20 twists.

    2 packages (8 ounces each) refrigerated
      Parker House dinner rolls
1½ cups shredded Cheddar cheese (6 ounces)
 ½ teaspoon oregano
 ¼ teaspoon crushed red pepper

1. Separate rolls into individual rectangles.
2. Combine cheese, oregano and red pepper; blend well. Sprinkle evenly over each rectangle.
3. Grasp top right hand corner and bottom left hand corner of rectangle; twist in opposite directions and stretch to an 8-inch length. Place on buttered cooky sheet, pressing ends down slightly.
4. Bake in a moderate oven (375°) for 12 minutes, or until golden brown. Serve warm with butter.

RIO GRANDE CORN MUFFINS
Seventeen minutes, from start to finish, is all it takes to make these peppy muffins.

Bake at 350° for 12 minutes. Makes 6 muffins.

    1 package (10 ounces) frozen corn muffins
 ½ cup shredded Muenster or Monterey Jack
      cheese (2 ounces)
    1 or 2 green chili peppers (from a 4-ounce can)

1. Place frozen muffins on a cooky sheet. Divide cheese evenly on tops of muffins.
2. Remove seeds from peppers; cut into 12 strips. Place 2 strips crisscross on each muffin.
3. Bake in a moderate oven (350°) 12 minutes, or until lightly browned. Serve immediately.

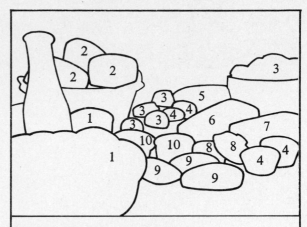

IDENTIFICATION OF BREADS SHOWN ON PAGES 36-37
1—Parmesan Garlic Bread; 2—Cheddar Cheese Bread; 3—Bacon Cheese Puffs; 4—Rio Grande Corn Muffins; 5—Swiss Batter Bread; 6—Cheese Cranberry Bread; 7—Cottage Cheese Fruit Bread; 8—Deviled Ham and Cheese Pinwheels; 9—Easy Cheese Boreks; 10—Little Dill Cheese Loaves. Recipes begin on page 34.

CHEDDAR WHOLE WHEAT BREAD
Make this in miniature-size loaves for serving with appetizers, or large ones for gift-giving.

Bake at 350° for 45 minutes for large loaf, 35 minutes for small. Makes 1 large whole wheat loaf or 6 miniature ones.

1¼ cups sifted all-purpose flour
 ½ cup sugar
    1 teaspoon baking powder
    1 teaspoon baking soda
    1 teaspoon salt
    2 cups shredded Cheddar cheese (8 ounces)
1¼ cups whole wheat flour
    1 cup chopped nuts
    1 tablespoon grated orange peel
    1 egg, slightly beaten
1¼ cups milk
 ¼ cup (½ stick) butter, melted
 ¼ cup light molasses

1. Sift together the flour, sugar, baking powder, baking soda and salt in a large bowl; add cheese, whole wheat flour, nuts and orange peel; blend all the ingredients thoroughly.
2. Combine egg, milk, butter and molasses; add all at once to sifted dry ingredients and stir only until blended. Spread evenly in large (9¼x5¼x 2¾-inch) loaf pan or 6 miniature-size loaf pans.
3. Bake in moderate oven (350°) 45 minutes for large loaf and 35 minutes for miniature loaves, or until cake tester inserted in center comes out clean. Allow to stand for 5 minutes; remove from pan onto wire rack to cool.
Variation: 1¼ cups sifted all-purpose flour may be substituted for the whole wheat flour.

Page 36: A bread board to beat all others! For an identification of the breads and muffins see the drawing above.

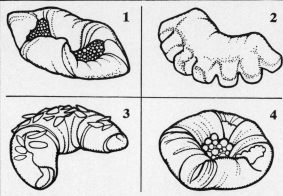

FOUR WAYS TO FOLD DANISH PASTRY

Start by cutting dough (See Cheese Danish recipe). **1.** Spoon filling onto squares. Overlap corners over filling. **2.** Spoon filling onto squares and spread to one edge; brush edges with egg; fold one edge over. Make slits in sealed edge; curve. **3.** Spoon filling onto one corner. Roll dough around filling; curve. Brush with egg, sprinkle with nuts. **4.** See Danish Pastry recipe.

DANISH PASTRY DOUGH

Start the day with a Cheese Danish, juice and milk or coffee!

Makes 2 large pastries, or about 24 individual pastries; or makes 1 large pastry and 12 individual pastries.

- **2 packages active dry yeast**
- **½ cup very warm water**
- **⅓ cup sugar**
- **¾ cup cold milk**
- **2 eggs**
- **4¼ cups sifted all-purpose flour**
- **1 teaspoon salt**
- **1 pound (4 sticks) unsalted butter**
- **Flour**

1. Sprinkle yeast into very warm water in a 1-cup measure. ("Very warm" water should feel comfortably warm when dropped on wrist.) Stir in ½ teaspoon of the sugar. Stir until yeast dissolves. Let stand undisturbed until bubbly and double in volume, about 10 minutes. Now you can tell the yeast is working.
2. Combine remaining sugar, milk, eggs, 3 cups of the flour, salt and the yeast mixture in large bowl. Beat, with electric mixer at medium speed, for 3 minutes (or beat with spoon, for 3 minutes). Beat in remaining flour with a wooden spoon until dough is shiny and elastic. Dough will be soft. Scrape down sides of bowl. Cover with plastic wrap. Refrigerate 30 minutes.
3. Place the sticks of butter 1 inch apart, between 2 sheets of wax paper; roll out to a 12-inch square. Chill on a cooky sheet until ready to use.
4. Sprinkle working surface heavily with flour, about ⅓ cup; turn dough out onto flour; sprinkle

Right: For a breakfast-tray special, try our Cheese-Danish, a light, flaky pastry with a cheese-and-jam filling. Recipe is on this page.

flour on top of dough. Roll out to an 18x13-inch rectangle. Brush off any excess flour very gently with a soft pastry brush.

5. Peel off top sheet of wax paper from butter; place butter paper side up on one end of dough to cover two-thirds of the dough; peel off remaining sheet of wax paper. For easy folding, carefully score butter lengthwise down center, without cutting into dough. Fold uncovered third of dough over middle third; brush off excess flour; then fold remaining third of dough over middle third to enclose butter completely. Turn dough clockwise so open side is away from you.

6. *Roll out to a 24x12-inch rectangle using enough flour to keep dough from sticking. Fold ends in to meet on center; then fold in half to make 4 layers. Turn again so open side is away from you. *Repeat rolling and folding this way 2 more times. Keep the dough to a perfect rectangle by rolling straight up and down and from side to side. When it is necessary, chill the dough between rollings. Clean off the working surface each time and dust lightly with flour. Refrigerate dough 1 hour or more (even overnight, if you wish, to relax dough and firm up butter layers). Cut dough in half, you can see the buttery layers, which when baked, become flaky and crisp. Work with only half the dough at a time. Keep the other half refrigerated until ready to use.

CHEESE DANISH

Bake at 400°, then 350° for 20 to 25 minutes. Makes 12 individual pastries.

- **½ Danish Pastry Dough**
  Cheese Filling (makes 1 cup): Combine 1 cup pot cheese, 1 egg yolk, ¼ cup sugar and 1 teaspoon grated lemon rind in container of electric blender; whirl until smooth.
  Cherry preserves
  Slightly beaten egg
- **½ cup corn syrup**

1. Roll pastry on floured surface to two 20x15-inch rectangles; trim edges even; with a sharp knife, cut into 12 five-inch squares.
2. Spoon Cheese Filling onto center of each square, dividing evenly; fold in all 4 corners to meet and overlap slightly in center to enclose filling completely; press points down with fingertip.
3. Place 2 inches apart on cooky sheet; let rise until double in bulk, about 30 minutes. Press down points again and fill center with a teaspoon of cherry preserves. Brush pastry with egg.
4. Place in hot oven (400°); lower heat immediately to 350°. Bake 20 to 25 minutes, or until puffed and golden brown. Heat corn syrup just until warm; brush over pastries. Remove to wire rack; cool. Add more preserves after pastries are baked, if you wish. Pastries will open up as they bake.

*NOTE: See illustrations in the left-hand column above for other folding techniques.

DEVILED HAM AND CHEESE PINWHEELS
Packaged buttermilk biscuits take the work out of these delicious morsels.

Bake at 450° for 10 minutes. Makes 16 pinwheels.

  1 can (2¼ ounces) deviled ham
  ½ cup shredded Swiss cheese (2 ounces)
  2 tablespoons butter, melted
  1 teaspoon freeze-dried chives
  2 packages (8 ounces each) refrigerated
    buttermilk biscuits

1. Combine ham, cheese, butter and chives in a small bowl; reserve.
2. On a lightly floured board, place 4 biscuits in a horizontal row overlapping each halfway; place 4 more biscuits in a row below and overlapping first row. Continue with remaining biscuits to form an 8-inch square.
3. Roll out with lightly floured rolling pin into a 10x16-inch rectangle. Press together any open spaces between the biscuits.
4. Spread ham and cheese filling evenly over rolled-out dough.
5. Roll up, lengthwise, jelly-roll fashion, keeping roll 16 inches long. Cut into 1-inch pieces with scissors or sharp knife. Tuck end of roll underneath pinwheel and place on lightly buttered cooky sheet.
6. Bake in a hot oven (450°) for 10 minutes, or until the pinwheels are lightly browned. Serve while still warm, with butter.

LITTLE DILL CHEESE LOAVES
Cottage cheese enhances the flavor of this simple-to-make yeast bread.

Bake at 350° for 45 minutes. Makes 6 individual loaves.

  1 package active dry yeast
  ½ cup very warm water
  1 cup (8 ounces) cream-style cottage cheese
  2 tablespoons sugar
  1 tablespoon instant minced onion
  2 teaspoons dillweed
  1 teaspoon salt
  ¼ teaspoon baking soda
  1 egg
  2⅓ cups sifted all-purpose flour
    Butter

1. Sprinkle yeast into very warm water in a large bowl. ("Very warm" water should feel comfortably warm when dropped on wrist.) Stir with spoon until the yeast dissolves.
2. Heat cheese just until lukewarm in small saucepan; stir into yeast mixture; add sugar, onion, dillweed, salt, baking soda, egg and 1⅓ cups flour. Beat with electric mixer at medium speed for 2 minutes. Stir in the remaining 1 cup of all-purpose flour to make a soft dough.

Right: The classic Dagwood, and all the ingredients that go into making this incredible sandwich. The recipe is on page 46.

3. Cover with a clean towel. Let rise in a warm place, away from draft, 1 hour, or until the dough is double in bulk.
4. Stir dough down; spoon evenly into six 6-ounce greased soufflé dishes or custard cups.
5. Let rise again in warm place, away from draft, 45 minutes, or until double in bulk.
6. Bake in moderate oven (350°) 30 minutes; cover with foil, then bake 15 minutes longer, or until loaves give a hollow sound when tapped. Brush tops with butter; remove from dishes to wire racks. Serve the loaves while still warm or cool completely, and serve with fresh butter.

CHEDDAR POPPY STRIPS
Golden brown and cheesy, these savory strips are topped with poppy seeds and butter.

Bake at 425° for 10 minutes. Makes 16 strips.

  2 cups buttermilk biscuit mix
  ½ teaspoon leaf basil, crumbled
  ½ cup milk
  2 tablespoons butter, melted
  4 ounces shredded Cheddar cheese (1 cup)
  1 teaspoon poppy seeds

1. Place biscuit mix in large bowl with basil. Stir in milk with fork until soft dough forms.
2. Knead dough a few times on floured board. Roll out into a 16x10-inch rectangle; brush with 1 tablespoon of the melted butter; sprinkle cheese evenly over dough.
3. Fold in thirds lengthwise. You will have a 16x3-inch strip.
4. Brush with remaining butter, sprinkle with poppy seeds; cut crosswise into 16 one-inch strips.
5. Place on ungreased cooky sheet. Bake in a hot oven (425°) 10 minutes, or until strips are golden brown. Serve warm.

HOT HERB BREAD STICKS
Better double this recipe for it's the kind of hot bread you just keep on eating.

Bake at 400° about 5 minutes. Makes 6 servings.

  6 tablespoons butter
  ¼ cup chopped parsley
  1 long thin loaf French bread
  2 tablespoons grated Parmesan cheese

1. Cream butter in small bowl; stir in parsley.
2. Cut bread crosswise into thirds, then split each third in half to make 6 pieces; score cut sides about 1 inch apart almost through to crusts.
3. Spread tops and into cuts generously with butter-parsley mixture; sprinkle with cheese; place on cooky sheet.
4. Bake in hot oven (400°) about 5 minutes, or until golden-crisp.

SWISS BATTER BREAD
Each slice of this loaf tastes teasingly of cheese.

Bake at 350° for 1 hour and 10 minutes. Makes 1 large loaf.

⅔ cup water
2 tablespoons sugar
3 teaspoons salt
1 tablespoon butter
1 small can evaporated milk (⅔ cup)
2 packages active dry yeast or
   2 cakes compressed yeast
⅔ cup very warm water
4½ cups sifted all-purpose flour
2 cups grated Swiss cheese (8 ounces)

1. Heat the ⅔ cup water with sugar, salt and butter just to boiling in a small saucepan; stir into evaporated milk in a small bowl; cool to lukewarm.
2. Sprinkle or crumble yeast into very warm water in a large bowl. ("Very warm" water should feel comfortably warm when dropped on wrist.) Stir until yeast dissolves, then stir in cooled milk.
3. Beat in 2 cups of the flour until almost smooth. Stir in cheese and remaining flour until well-blended, then beat vigorously with a spoon, scraping down side of bowl often, 20 strokes, or until dough is very stiff.
4. Cover with a clean towel; let rise in a warm place, away from draft, 45 minutes, or until the dough is double in bulk.
5. Stir dough down; beat again about 10 strokes; spoon into a greased 8-cup round baking dish. Cover; let rise again, 30 minutes, or until not quite double in bulk.
6. Bake in lower ⅓ of moderate oven (350°) 1 hour and 10 minutes, or until bread gives a hollow sound when tapped. (If bread starts to get too brown, cover it lightly with foil during last 30 minutes of baking.) Remove from dish; cool.

BACON-CHEESE PUFFS
A cube of sharp Cheddar melts in the center of each tender muffin as it bakes.

Bake at 400° for 25 minutes. Makes 12 muffins.

2 cups biscuit mix
5 slices crisp bacon, crumbled
¾ cup milk
1 egg
12 cubes Cheddar cheese (4 ounces)

1. Combine biscuit mix and crumbled bacon in a medium-size bowl; add milk and egg. Stir just to mix.
2. Spoon half of batter into 12 greased medium-size muffin-pan cups. Press a cheese cube into each muffin cup. Evenly spoon remaining batter over cheese, covering cheese completely.
3. Bake in hot oven (400°) 25 minutes, or until golden. Serve hot.

CHEESE CRANBERRY BREAD
This bread is particularly popular at holiday time.

Bake at 350° for 1 hour and 15 minutes. Makes 1 loaf.

2 cups fresh or frozen cranberries
2 cups all-purpose flour
1 cup sugar
1 tablespoon baking powder
½ teaspoon salt
1½ cups shredded Cheddar cheese (6 ounces)
½ cup coarsely chopped walnuts
1 cup milk
1 egg, slightly beaten
¼ cup (½ stick) butter, melted
1 tablespoon grated orange peel

1. Halve the cranberries; set aside for Step 2.
2. Sift flour, sugar, baking powder and salt in a bowl. Add berries, cheese and nuts; toss.
3. Combine milk, egg, butter and orange peel; add to flour mixture all at once. Stir only until all dry ingredients are moistened. Turn into buttered loaf pan (9x5x2¾).
4. Bake in moderate oven (350°) 1 hour and 15 minutes, or until pick inserted in middle comes out clean. Allow to stand 10 minutes. Turn out of pan onto wire rack to cool.

COTTAGE CHEESE FRUIT BREAD
A quick bread that's delicious for breakfast.

Bake at 350° for 50 to 60 minutes. Makes 2 medium-size loaves or 1 large loaf.

6 tablespoons (¾ stick) butter, softened
½ cup firmly packed light brown sugar
2 eggs
1 tablespoon grated lemon peel
1 tablespoon grated orange peel
1½ cups cottage cheese
2 cups all-purpose flour
2 teaspoons baking powder
¾ teaspoon baking soda
¾ teaspoon salt
1 cup finely chopped dried apricots
½ cup chopped pecans

1. Cream butter in a large mixing bowl; add sugar gradually, beating well until light and fluffy. Add eggs, one at a time, beating well after each addition. Add fruit peels and cottage cheese; beat.
2. Mix flour, baking powder, soda and salt; add to butter-egg mixture. Mix just until blended. Fold in apricots and nuts. Turn into two buttered (7⅜x3⅝x2¼-inch) loaf pans or one (9x5x3-inch) loaf pan.
3. Bake in a moderate oven (350°) for 50 minutes for medium-size loaves, and 1 hour for large loaf, or until cake tester inserted in middle comes out clean. Turn loaves onto wire rack to cool.

BIG BURGERS & PIZZAS

THE FAMILY CIRCLE BIG BURGER
It's a delicious mouthful!

Makes 6 servings.

½ cup mayonnaise or salad dressing
¼ cup chili sauce
¼ cup chopped green pepper
1 teaspoon instant minced onion
2 pounds ground round
2 teaspoons salt
¼ teaspoon pepper
2 tablespoons butter
6 slices Cheddar cheese (about 6 ounces)
1 large dill pickle, cut into 12 slices
6 thin tomato slices
1 small onion, peeled and sliced thinly
1½ cups finely shredded lettuce (¼ small head)
9 split hamburger buns, or 6 high hamburger buns or soft buns, split into thirds, toasted

1. Combine mayonnaise or salad dressing, chili sauce, green pepper and instant minced onion in a small bowl; mix well. Reserve for Step 6.
2. Mix ground round lightly with salt and pepper. Shape into 12 thin patties.
3. Pan-fry 6 burgers in part of butter over medium heat in a large skillet 3 minutes on each side for rare, or until meat is done as you like it.
4. Place a slice of cheese on each of the burgers and broil, 4 inches from heat, about 2 minutes, or just until cheese melts slightly. Pan-fry the remaining hamburgers in remaining butter in same skillet.
5. To assemble: Place the cheeseburgers on the bottom halves of 6 hamburger buns; top each with 2 dill-pickle slices. Place split buns on the top.
6. Top buns with remaining hamburgers, then tomato and onion slices and ¼ cup shredded lettuce. Spread 2 tablespoons of the prepared sauce on the cut top portion of the buns. Place over the lettuce. Secure with a toothpick or wooden skewer.

THE WELSHMAN
Have a cheeseburger a different way.

Makes 4 servings.

2 cups shredded Cheddar cheese (8 ounces)
2 teaspoons all-purpose flour
¼ cup beer
1 teaspoon Worcestershire sauce
¼ teaspoon dry mustard
1 pound ground round or chuck
1 teaspoon salt
⅛ teaspoon pepper
2 tablespoons butter
4 hamburger rolls, split, toasted and buttered

1. Toss cheese with flour. Heat beer in a medium-size saucepan over very low heat. Add Worcestershire, mustard, cheese; stir until cheese melts.
2. Season beef with salt and pepper; shape ground beef into 4 patties, about the size of the rolls.
3. Melt butter in a large skillet. Pan-fry hamburgers about 4 minutes on each side, or until done as you like them. Place on bottoms of rolls.
4. Spoon cheese mixture over burgers. Top each with remaining halves of rolls. Garnish with red-pepper slices, if you wish.

PIZZA RUSTICA
A two-crust melt-in-the-mouth pizza brimming with 4 cheeses, spinach and salami. And not a tomato in sight!

Bake at 375° for 1 hour. Makes two 9-inch pizzas.

1 package (10 ounces) chopped frozen spinach, cooked and drained
1 container (15½ ounces) ricotta cheese
1 cup shredded mozzarella cheese (4 ounces)
¼ cup grated provolone cheese (1 ounce)
¼ cup grated Parmesan cheese (1 ounce)
¼ pound Italian salami, chopped (1 cup)
2 eggs, lightly beaten
1 teaspoon salt
¼ teaspoon ground nutmeg
⅛ teaspoon pepper
2 cups sifted all-purpose flour
1 teaspoon salt
½ cup (1 stick) butter, softened
½ cup vegetable shortening
3 eggs, lightly beaten

1. Combine spinach, cheeses, salami, 2 eggs, salt, nutmeg and pepper in medium-size bowl; reserve.
2. Sift flour and salt into a large bowl; cut in butter and shortening with a pastry blender until mixture is crumbly. Reserve 2 tablespoons of egg; add remaining eggs to flour mixture. Mix lightly with fork just until pastry holds together and leaves side of bowl clean. Divide dough into 4 equal parts.
3. Roll out ¼ of the dough to a 12-inch round on a lightly floured pastry board; fit into a 9-inch pie plate; trim overhang to ½ inch.
4. Roll out another ¼ of the dough to an 11-inch round; cut slits near center to let steam escape; spoon half of spinach filling into pastry shell. Cover filling with rolled out dough. Trim overhang to ½ inch; turn edges under, flush with rim; flute. Make the second pie in same way with remaining dough.
5. Combine reserved egg with 1 tablespoon water in a 1-cup measure; brush on pies.
6. Bake in moderate oven (375°) for one hour, or until bubbly-hot and golden-brown.

Our smorgasbord of sandwiches includes, from top to bottom on opposite page: Stuffed Ham Slices, Blue Cheese Open-Face Sandwich with egg wedges, Beef Roll-ups, and two more blue cheese sandwiches with egg and apple garnishes. On this page, Ham, Swiss & Asparagus Rollups, Blue Cheese Open-Face with shrimp garnish, Hero Boy Special and Gouda-Bacon Muffin. Recipes are in this chapter.

LUNCH & DINNER SANDWICHES

POCKETBOOK HOT DOGS
The "rolls" are made from ready-to-use biscuit mix.

Bake at 450° for 12 minutes. Makes 4 servings.

2 cups biscuit mix
   Milk
1 cup shredded Cheddar cheese (4 ounces)
4 frankfurters
4 slices bacon, cooked and crumbled
2 tablespoons butter
2 tablespoons prepared mustard

1. Prepare biscuit mix with milk, following label directions for rolled biscuits; stir in ⅓ cup of the Cheddar cheese.
2. Turn dough out onto a lightly floured pastry cloth or board; knead several times, or until smooth. Pat out to a rectangle, 6x5; cut crosswise into 4 pieces. Place on a cooky sheet.
3. Bake in very hot oven (450°) 12 minutes, or until golden. Remove from oven; raise temperature to BROIL.
4. While biscuits bake, heat frankfurters in water, following label directions; drain. Mix remaining cheese and bacon in a small bowl.
5. Split biscuits lengthwise almost through; spread with butter, then mustard. Place a frankfurter in each biscuit; sprinkle with bacon mixture. Return to cooky sheet.
6. Broil, 4 to 5 inches from heat, 1 minute, or until cheese melts. Serve hot.

HAM, SWISS AND ASPARAGUS ROLL-UPS
This knife-and-fork open-face sandwich offers lots of good flavor and nutrition.

Bake at 375° for 5 minutes. Makes 8 sandwiches.

8 slices white bread
8 slices cooked ham
8 slices Swiss cheese
8 asparagus spears, cooked

1. Toast bread slices lightly on both sides. Place one ham slice on each piece of toast. Place one asparagus spear on top of each cheese slice. Roll cheese slice up around asparagus and place on top of ham slices and bread.
2. Bake in a moderate oven (375°) about 5 minutes, or just until cheese melts. Serve on a large platter or individual plates, while still warm.

SOME CHEESE FILLINGS THAT FREEZE WELL
- Cream cheese and chopped stuffed olives moistened with milk.
- Mashed sardines, lemon juice and grated cheese.
- Sliced tongue and Cheddar cheese with mustard pickle.
- Sliced meat loaf, sliced Swiss cheese and mustard.
- Ground cooked ham, shredded Cheddar cheese, minced onion and chili sauce.
- Chopped cooked chicken, chopped salted almonds and cream cheese softened with milk.
- Cream cheese and blue cheese (equal parts) moistened with milk.

DAGWOOD SANDWICH
It's made with memories of midnight raids on the icebox!

Makes 6 to 8 servings.

1 round loaf white bread, about 12 inches in diameter
¼ cup (½ stick) butter, softened or
   ¼ cup mayonnaise
½ pound sliced roast beef
½ pound sliced Muenster cheese
½ pound sliced bologna
1 pint cherry tomatoes or
   1 large tomato, sliced
½ pound sliced salami
1 pound Swiss cheese slices
½ pound cooked ham slices
1 head lettuce

1. Cut bread into 3 horizontal slices; spread each slice with softened butter or mayonnaise.
2. Arrange roast beef, Muenster cheese, bologna and tomatoes on one slice of bread. Top with second slice of bread.
3. Arrange salami, Swiss cheese, ham and lettuce on top of second slice. Top with third slice of bread. If necessary, fasten with picks before slicing.

TUNA HOBOS
Bits of mild cheese melt through the tuna-salad filling.

Bake at 400° for 20 minutes. Makes 4 servings.

1 can (about 7 ounces) tuna, drained and flaked
¼ cup diced celery
1 cup diced Swiss cheese (4 ounces)
1 tablespoon chopped parsley
1 pimiento, diced
¼ cup mayonnaise or salad dressing
1 teaspoon lemon juice
½ teaspoon salt
½ teaspoon Worcestershire sauce
4 split hamburger buns, buttered

1. Combine tuna, celery, cheese, parsley and pimiento in a medium-size bowl.
2. Blend mayonnaise or salad dressing with lemon juice, salt and Worcestershire sauce in a cup; spoon over tuna mixture; toss lightly to mix.
3. Put hamburger buns together with filling, dividing evenly. Wrap in foil; place on cooky sheet.
4. Bake in hot oven (400°) 20 minutes, or until heated through. Remove sandwiches from foil.

BEEF ROLL-UPS
These sandwiches offer all kinds of ingredients.

Makes 6 sandwiches.

  8 ounces cream cheese, softened
  1 envelope (.7 ounces) onion salad dressing mix
  1 tablespoon prepared horseradish
  1 to 2 tablespoons milk
18 thin slices roast beef
12 thin carrot sticks
12 large slices dark rye bread
  ¼ cup (½ stick) butter, softened
  6 lettuce leaves
  6 slices Swiss cheese

1. Blend cream cheese, salad dressing mix, horseradish and milk in a medium-size bowl. Spread about 1 tablespoon of the mixture on each roast beef slice. Place a carrot stick at one end of each roast beef slice; roll, jelly-roll fashion: set aside.
2. Butter bread slices and then layer 6 of them with lettuce leaves, Swiss cheese and beef roll-ups (3 on each slice). Top with remaining 6 slices bread. Cut each in half; wrap, chill, or serve immediately.

HERO BOY SPECIALS
It's beef topped with tomato slices and cheese.

Bake at 400° for 35 minutes. Makes 8 servings.

  1 pound ground beef
  1 can (8 ounces) tomato sauce
  ¼ cup finely chopped onion
  ¾ teaspoon salt
  ¾ teaspoon oregano, crushed
    Generous dash pepper
  2 teaspoons Worcestershire sauce
  ½ cup dry bread crumbs
  4 hero rolls, split lengthwise and toasted
16 tomato slices (2 medium-size tomatoes)
24 square slices sharp Cheddar cheese

1. Combine the ground beef, tomato sauce, onion, salt, oregano, pepper, Worcestershire sauce and bread crumbs in a large bowl; mix well.
2. Spread meat mixture evenly onto toasted roll halves, covering edges completely.
3. Place on cooky sheet and bake in a hot oven (400°) for 30 minutes. Top each roll with 2 tomato slices and 3 cheese slices. Return to oven about 5 minutes, or just until cheese melts.

GOUDA-BACON MUFFINS
This open-face sandwich is a good choice for brunch.

Makes 4 sandwiches.

2 onion-flavor English muffins
8 slices Canadian bacon, cooked
8 ounces Gouda cheese
1 red apple, sliced

1. Split muffins in half and toast. Place 2 slices cooked bacon on each muffin.
2. Cut cheese into 12 wedges or slices; arrange 3 wedges on each muffin; top with apple slice.

BLUE CHEESE OPEN-FACE SANDWICHES
Top this spread with almost any favorite garnish.

Makes 10 sandwiches.

  1 cup crumbled blue cheese (4 ounces)
  1 cup butter, softened
10 slices rye bread
    Garnishes (see below)

Blend blue cheese and butter together in a medium-size bowl until fluffy. Spread over slices of bread. Decorate each sandwich in any of these ways:
1. Top with apple wedges dipped in lemon juice.
2. Top with sieved egg yolk and red caviar.
3. Top with three hard-cooked egg wedges.
4. Top with three cooked, shelled, deveined shrimp.
Chill all prepared sandwiches at least 30 minutes.

STUFFED HAM SLICES
A crusty loaf with a ham-cheese-pickle core.

Makes 16 sandwiches.

1 loaf unsliced Italian bread (about 18 inches long)
¼ cup mayonnaise or salad dressing
⅓ cup chopped parsley
8 ounces cream cheese
¾ cup very finely chopped celery
2 tablespoons very finely chopped onion
¼ teaspoon salt
2 packages (4 ounces each) sliced boiled ham
1 large dill pickle

1. Split bread lengthwise; hollow out each half with a fork, leaving a ½-inch-thick shell. (Save insides to make a crumb topping for a casserole.)
2. Spread mayonnaise or salad dressing over hollows in loaf; sprinkle parsley over mayonnaise.
3. Blend cream cheese, celery, onion and salt in a bowl; spoon into bread halves, packing down well and leaving a small hollow down center.
4. Quarter pickle lengthwise; roll each quarter inside a double-thick slice of ham. Place rolls, end to end, in center of bottom half of loaf; cover with remaining half of bread. Wrap tightly; chill.
5. To serve, cut into 16 slices. Garnish with parsley.

TEA SANDWICHES

ASPARAGUS ROLLS
Asparagus spears are tucked in each sandwich.

Makes about 4 dozen.

 2 bunches fresh asparagus (about 4 pounds)
 Bottled thin French dressing
1½ pounds (24 ounces) cream cheese
 6 tablespoons (¾ stick) butter
48 slices soft white bread (from 3 loaves)

1. Break tough woody ends from asparagus; wash stalks well. If scales are large or sandy, cut off with a sharp knife, then wash stalks again. Cut off flowery tip of each stalk to a 3-inch length to use for sandwiches; chill remaining for another day.
2. Tie stalks in two or three bundles; stand up in a pan. Pour in boiling water to one inch; cover.
3. Cook 15 minutes, or just until crisply tender. Lift out bundles; drain; snip off strings. Place asparagus in a large shallow dish; brush with French dressing; chill several hours to season.
4. Put cheese and butter in a bowl; beat well.
5. Trim crusts from bread; roll each slice thin with a rolling pin; spread with cheese mixture. Place a seasoned asparagus spear at one end of each slice; roll up tightly, jelly-roll fashion. Wrap and chill.

DATE-NUT ORANGE ROUNDS
Use the cheese-orange spread for dessert, too.

Makes 30 sandwiches.

1 loaf (16 ounces) date-nut bread
8 ounces cream cheese, softened
2 tablespoons grated orange rind

1. Using a round cooky or hors d'oeuvres cutter, cut 2 rounds from each slice of bread.
2. Combine softened cream cheese and 1 tablespoon of the orange rind. Spread on bread.
3. Decorate edge of each with remaining rind.

CREAM CHEESE MIMOSA TEA SANDWICHES
Make these ahead of time and store in the refrigerator.

Makes 24 sandwiches.

12 square slices dark pumpernickel bread
 8 ounces cream cheese, softened
 6 hard-cooked egg yolks, sieved
24 pimiento-stuffed green olive slices

1. Using an oval-shaped cooky or sandwich cutter (2 inches long), cut 2 ovals from each slice of bread.
2. Spread each slice with the softened cream cheese; sprinkle tops with sieved egg yolk. Top each with an olive slice, as shown on page 48.

DEVILED HAM OPEN-FACE SANDWICHES
You can put these hors d'oeuvres together in a jiffy.

Makes about 32 sandwiches.

16 slices white bread (about 1 pound loaf)
 2 cans (2¼ ounces each) deviled ham
 3 ounces cream cheese, softened
 Cucumber slices
 Pimiento cut-outs

1. Trim crusts from bread slices; cut hearts or other decorative shapes from the slices, using 2-inch cooky or hors d'oeuvres cutters.
2. Combine ham and cream cheese until well blended; spread on bread cut-outs. Decorate with cucumber and pimiento as shown on page 48.

PUMPERNICKEL-CREAM CHEESE ALTERNATES
Dark and white bread are used to assemble these.

Makes 20 tea sandwiches.

10 square slices dark pumpernickel bread
 5 slices white sandwich bread
 1 pound (16 ounces) cream cheese, softened
 1 cup finely chopped parsley

1. Trim crusts from bread slices. Combine softened cheese and parsley until well blended. Spread cheese mixture over bread slices.
2. Assemble sandwiches: Place a slice of white bread between 2 slices of pumpernickel bread. Carefully cut assembled sandwiches into quarters.

STRAWBERRY PINWHEELS
Use fresh unsliced bread for these tea sandwiches.

Makes 6 to 7 dozen pinwheels.

1 pound (16 ounces) cream cheese
2 cups strawberries, washed, hulled and sliced
2 tablespoons 10X (confectioners' powdered) sugar
1 loaf unsliced white bread

1. Soften cream cheese in medium-size bowl; blend in strawberries and sugar until smooth.
2. Cut crusts from loaf of bread, then slice bread lengthwise into 9 or 10 thin slices; cover with a dampened towel; let stand 10 minutes.
3. Spread slices, 1 at a time, with cheese mixture, using 3 to 4 tablespoonfuls per slice; roll up, jelly-roll fashion; wrap tightly in wax paper; chill.
4. Unwrap and slice rolls crosswise into pinwheels.

Left—on tea tray: Date-Nut Orange Rounds, Deviled Ham Open-Face Sandwiches and Strawberry Pinwheels. On table: Pumpernickel-Cream Cheese Alternates, Cream Cheese Mimosa Tea Sandwiches and Asparagus Rolls. Recipes are in this chapter.

Next page: Bread snacks to serve as pre-dinner tidbits. Recipes for bread sticks are in this chapter.

4
ONE-POT SPECIALS

One pot is all it takes to whip up some truly scrumptious cheese dishes. The one pot can be a fondue, brimming with melted cheese and wine. It can be a casserole, filled with an inviting combination of cheese, pasta, vegetables, meat and seasonings. Or, it can be that old standby, the soup pot, and here the possibilities are almost unlimited. In this chapter we include recipes for all, plus a selection of cheese sauces to enhance main-dish and dessert offerings.

FONDUES

Fondue comes from a French word meaning "to melt," generally translated as a preparation of melted cheese flavored with wine or brandy. But it can also be a meat dish cooked in hot oil and served with a variety of sauces, or a vegetable offering that's cooked in hot broth. On these pages we stick to the cheese fondue, and even our sampling of recipes is only a beginning. You can make fondue with almost any kind of cheese and serve it with bread, meat, fish, vegetable dippers or fresh fruit. Following are some pointers you should know when preparing cheese fondue.

• Use a flameproof earthenware fondue pot or a chafing dish, and have plenty of napkins and long-handled forks on hand.

• Light the fondue burner a few moments before making the fondue. (And, if you wish, make the fondue at the range and then whisk it immediately into the fondue pot; it's faster this way.)

• Shred the cheese ahead of time and store in refrigerator. It melts more uniformly and more quickly when shredded. Add the shredded cheese to the fondue mixture by the handful, stirring constantly, and keeping heat low.

• If fondue becomes too thick on standing, add a little warmed liquid of same type used in recipe you're following. Keep heat low so fondue stays warm, but does not boil.

• When you reach the bottom of the pot, you'll notice a golden crust of cheese has formed around the edges. This should be lifted out and enjoyed as a special treat.

• What to drink with fondue? Purists recommend hot tea, but you can drink anything you like, except water.

CREAM CHEESE FONDUE
Vegetable dippers are a nice contrast to the delightful saltiness of this fondue.

Makes 6 to 8 servings.

1½   pounds (24 ounces) cream cheese, cubed
1¾   cups milk
  1   tablespoon prepared mustard
 ¼   cup capers, drained
  1   can (2 ounces) anchovy fillets, drained and chopped
     Vegetable dippers such as carrot sticks, celery stalks and lettuce wedges

1. Combine cubed cream cheese and milk in a medium-size saucepan. Cook over medium heat, stirring constantly, until the cream cheese is melted and well blended with the milk.

2. Add mustard, capers and chopped anchovies. Continue cooking, for about 5 minutes, or until fondue is hot. Transfer to fondue dish and serve with vegetable dippers such as carrot sticks and celery.

SWISS FONDUE
One of the world's most sociable foods—it's even entertaining to eat.

Makes 6 servings.

6   cups grated Swiss cheese (1½ pounds)
3   tablespoons all-purpose flour
1   clove garlic, halved
2   cups dry white wine
3   tablespoons kirsch
   Paprika
1   loaf Italian bread

1. Toss the grated Swiss cheese with all-purpose flour in a large bowl.

2. Rub cut ends of garlic around bottom and side of a fondue dish or large heavy frying pan; pour the wine into the pan.

3. Heat very slowly just until bubbles start to rise from bottom of pan.

4. Stir in cheese mixture, a small amount at a time, with a wooden spoon. (Wait to add more until all of one addition has melted. Do not let mixture boil at any time.)

5. Stir in kirsch. If frying pan is used for cooking, pour fondue into a heated chafing dish or fondue pot to keep the mixture hot while serving; sprinkle with paprika.

6. Cut bread into small pieces, leaving some crust on each; place in a basket. Set out fondue or regular forks so everyone can spear a piece of bread on fork, then twirl into the simmering cheese sauce.

CHEDDAR-DRIED BEEF FONDUE
If you have any of this fondue left over, reheat it another day and serve on toast. Add a salad and you have a complete lunch or light dinner.

Makes about 4½ cups fondue.

2   cans (10¾ ounces each) condensed cream of mushroom soup
4   cups grated sharp Cheddar cheese (16 ounces)
¼   cup all-purpose flour
1   tablespoon Worcestershire sauce
1   jar (5 ounces) sliced dried beef, chopped (about 2 cups)

1. Heat soup over medium heat in a large saucepan just until it bubbles.

2. Lower heat; add cheese gradually, stirring constantly, until melted. Add Worcestershire sauce and dried beef. Cook just until thoroughly heated.

3. Pour fondue into cheese fondue pot or chafing dish; serve with vegetable dippers.

Page 53: Sausage Lasagna almost demands second helpings. Serve it with wine, a salad and our Cheddar Cheese Twists. Recipe for the lasagna is on page 59, for the bread sticks, on page 35.

Right: Chili-Tortilla Casserole served with shredded lettuce, avocado and grated Parmesan. Recipe is on page 62.

MACARONI-CHEDDAR PUFF

All you do is add egg yolks and whites to macaroni and cheese and it comes out as puffy and light as a classic soufflé.

Bake at 300° for 1 hour. Makes 6 servings.

1 cup uncooked elbow macaroni (2 cups cooked)
6 tablespoons (¾ stick) butter
6 tablespoons all-purpose flour
2 teaspoons dry mustard
1 teaspoon salt
1½ cups milk
1 tablespoon Worcestershire sauce
1½ cups grated Cheddar cheese (6 ounces)
6 eggs, separated

1. Cook macaroni, following label directions; drain; cool; reserve for Step 4.
2. Melt butter in a medium-size saucepan; stir in flour, mustard and salt; cook, stirring constantly, until bubbly. Stir in milk and Worcestershire sauce; continue cooking and stirring until sauce thickens and boils 1 minute. Stir in cheese until melted; remove from heat. Let cool while beating eggs.
3. Beat egg whites just until they form soft peaks in a medium-size bowl.
4. Beat egg yolks until creamy-thick in a large bowl; beat in cheese sauce very slowly. Fold in egg whites until no streaks of white remain; fold in the reserved macaroni.
5. Spoon into a greased 8-cup soufflé dish or straight-side baking dish; gently cut a deep circle in mixture about 1 inch in from edge with a rubber spatula. (This gives the puff its high crown.)
6. Bake in slow oven (300°) 1 hour, or until puffy-firm and golden. Serve at once.

SAUSAGE LASAGNA

Make lots of this because everyone will be back for second helpings!

Bake at 350° for 35 minutes. Makes 12 servings.

2 cloves garlic, crushed
3 tablespoons olive oil
2 cans (15 ounces each) tomato sauce
2 cans (6 ounces each) tomato paste
1 cup water
2 bay leaves
1 teaspoon sugar
1 teaspoon salt
½ teaspoon pepper
4 cups ricotta cheese (2 pounds)
2 eggs
1 package (1 pound) lasagne noodles, cooked and drained
1 pound sweet Italian sausages, cooked and sliced
1 pound hot Italian sausages, cooked and sliced
1½ pounds sliced mozzarella cheese
½ cup grated Parmesan and Romano cheese (2 ounces)

1. In a large kettle, sauté garlic in oil until golden. Add tomato sauce, tomato paste, water, bay leaves, sugar, salt and pepper. Cover; simmer, stirring frequently, for 25 minutes.
2. Combine ricotta cheese and eggs in a large bowl; stir until well blended.
3. Assemble lasagna: Spoon about ½ cup of sauce onto the bottom of a 13x9x2-inch baking dish. Arrange ⅓ of the cooked noodles over the sauce; spoon on ⅓ of the ricotta cheese mixture, ⅓ of the sausage slices and ⅓ of the mozzarella slices. Repeat layers until all ingredients are used, ending with mozzarella slices and any extra sauce.
4. Bake in a moderate oven (350°) 35 minutes, or until bubbly. Cool 15 minutes; cut into squares. Serve with Parmesan and Romano cheese.

VENETIAN MANICOTTI

Three kinds of cheese blend in this meatless version of an Italian favorite.

Bake at 350° for 1 hour. Makes 8 servings.

1 package (12 ounces) manicotti noodles
2 cups (1 pound) cream-style cottage cheese
8 ounces cream cheese
2 packages (9 ounces each) frozen chopped spinach, thawed and drained
2 eggs
2 teaspoons salt
1 teaspoon Italian seasoning
Dash of pepper
6 tablespoons (¾ stick) butter
6 tablespoons all-purpose flour
1 teaspoon dry mustard
4 cups milk
4 cups grated Cheddar cheese (1 pound)

1. Cook manicotti noodles, a few at a time, in a large amount of boiling salted water, following label directions; lift out carefully with a slotted spoon so as not to break them; place in cold water.
2. Mix cottage and cream cheeses, one package of the spinach, eggs, 1 teaspoon of the salt, Italian seasoning and pepper until well blended in a medium-size bowl. Place remaining package of spinach in a small bowl and set aside for Step 4.
3. Melt butter in a medium-size saucepan; stir in flour, remaining 1 teaspoon salt and mustard; cook, stirring constantly, just until bubbly. Stir in milk; continue cooking and stirring until sauce thickens and boils 1 minute; remove from heat. Stir in grated cheese until melted.
4. Blend 1 cup of the sauce into spinach in bowl; spoon into a baking dish, 13x9x2, to make a layer.
5. Lift manicotti noodles, one at a time, from water; drain well. Fill with cottage-cheese mixture, using a long-handle spoon; place in rows in a single layer over spinach mixture in dish. Spoon remaining cheese sauce over and around noodles.
6. Bake in moderate oven (350°) 1 hour, or until the casserole is bubbly-hot.

Left: Hale and Hearty Cheese Soup, a blend of cheese, fish and vegetables, is a quick main-dish idea that watches the budget. The recipe is on page 68.

Left: Serve
Chicken
Cordon Bleu
En
Casserole
for your
next
buffet dinner.
It's a
portable
main dish
made
with ham,
broccoli,
Swiss cheese
and rice.
Recipe is on
page 64.

61

CHILI-TORTILLA CASSEROLE
A big, quick supper casserole with hot-pungent Mexican flavors cooled down a bit for family fare.

Bake at 400° for 15 minutes. Makes 6 servings.

8 frozen tortillas, from a 9-ounce package
1 pound ground beef
1 can (14½ ounces) sliced baby tomatoes
1 can (8 ounces) tomato sauce
1 envelope (2¼ ounces) chili sauce mix
1 can (15 ounces) red kidney beans
1 can (12 ounces) whole-kernel corn
½ cup pitted ripe olives
1 cup grated Cheddar cheese (4 ounces)
Shredded lettuce
Sliced avocado

1. Preheat oven to 400°. Remove the frozen tortillas from package to thaw. (Return remaining tortillas to freezer for later.)
2. Brown meat in a large skillet. Stir in tomatoes, tomato sauce and chili sauce mix. Simmer, uncovered, 5 minutes. Stir in beans, corn and olives. Cut tortillas into quarters.
3. Layer meat mixture and tortillas in a 2-quart casserole, ending with tortillas. Sprinkle with cheese.
4. Bake in hot oven (400°) 15 minutes, or until bubbly hot and cheese is melted. Garnish with shredded lettuce and avocado on top. Serve with additional lettuce and avocado, if you wish.

TUNA FLORENTINE
A deliciously mellow cheese sauce adds the perfect touch to this easy casserole.

Bake at 350° for 25 minutes. Makes 8 servings.

6 tablespoons (¾ stick) butter
1 medium-size onion, chopped (½ cup)
¼ cup all-purpose flour
½ teaspoon salt
Dash nutmeg
2 cups milk
1½ cups shredded Swiss cheese (6 ounces)
2 cans (7 ounces each) tuna, drained and flaked
2 packages (10 ounces each) frozen chopped spinach, thawed and drained
½ cup fine dry bread crumbs
¼ cup grated Parmesan cheese

1. Melt butter in a medium-size saucepan; sauté onion just until soft; stir in flour; salt and nutmeg; cook, stirring constantly, just until bubbly. Stir in milk; continue cooking and stirring until sauce thickens and bubbles 1 minute; remove from heat. Stir in shredded cheese, just until melted; add tuna.
2. Place spinach in the bottom of a lightly greased 6-cup baking dish; spoon tuna-cheese mixture over the top; top with crumbs and Parmesan cheese.
3. Bake in moderate oven (350°) 25 minutes, or until top of casserole is golden.

VEAL PARMIGIANA AND GREEN NOODLE BAKE
Two Italian favorites team in this one-dish dinner. It's colorful and quick, too, thanks to frozen foods.

Bake at 375° for 15 minutes. Makes 4 servings.

1 package (8 ounces) green noodles
1 can condensed cream of mushroom soup
½ cup dairy sour cream
2 tablespoons milk
8 ounces whipped cream cheese
½ cup grated Parmesan cheese (2 ounces)
¼ cup (½ stick) butter, melted
1 can (3 or 4 ounces) sliced mushrooms, undrained
4 frozen breaded veal patties (about 1¼ pounds)
3 tablespoons butter
2 canned pimientos, slivered
8 ounces mozzarella cheese
½ cup canned meatless spaghetti sauce

1. Cook noodles, following label directions; drain.
2. Meanwhile, blend soup with sour cream, milk, cream cheese, Parmesan and melted butter; stir in mushrooms and their liquid. Set aside.
3. Quickly brown veal patties on both sides in butter in a skillet. Drain on toweling; cut in half.
4. Drain noodles. Combine with soup mixture and pimiento; turn into shallow 12-cup baking dish. Arrange veal patty halves on top. Cut mozzarella into 8 slices; top each patty with one slice. Spoon spaghetti sauce in center of each cheese slice. Bake in a moderate over (375°) 15 minutes, or until cheese melts. Garnish with clusters of parsley.

OLD ENGLISH CASSEROLE
The cheese topping adds a lively touch.

Bake at 350° for 30 minutes. Makes 6 servings.

1 package (8 ounces) noodles, cooked and drained
1½ pounds ground beef
1 large onion, thinly sliced
1 tablespoon all-purpose flour
½ teaspoon seasoned salt
¼ teaspoon lemon pepper
1 can (3 or 4 ounces) sliced mushrooms
1 can (1 pound) green beans, drained
1 can (15 ounces) tomato sauce
1 cup grated Cheddar cheese (4 ounces)

1. Place noodles in a greased 8-cup baking dish.
2. Brown beef in a large skillet; remove meat to a bowl; drain all but 1 tablespoon fat from skillet. Sauté onion in fat until tender in skillet; return beef.
3. Blend in flour, seasoned salt and lemon pepper. Stir in sliced mushrooms and liquid, green beans and tomato sauce. Spoon mixture over noodles, spreading evenly; sprinkle with cheese.
4. Bake in moderate oven (350°) 30 minutes.

Right: Some of the ingredients found in Country Cheese Dip, a delicious fondue you serve with either bread, cocktail franks, fresh vegetables—or all three! Recipe is on page 56.

PEPPERONI AND CHICK PEA CASSEROLE

This is a robust Italian meal-in-one done the easy American way.

Bake at 375° for one hour. Makes 6 servings.

    2 pepperoni sausages, sliced thin
    1 cup frozen chopped onion
    ½ cup frozen chopped green pepper
    1 clove garlic, crushed
    1 tablespoon parsley flakes
    ½ teaspoon leaf oregano, crumbled
    ¼ teaspoon leaf basil, crumbled
      Pinch of salt
    2 cans (8 ounces each) tomato sauce
    ½ cup dry red or white wine
    2 tablespoons brown sugar
    2 cans (1 pound, 4 ounces each) chick peas,
      well-drained
    ½ cup shredded Cheddar cheese (2 ounces)

1. Brown pepperoni lightly in a large skillet 2 to 3 minutes. Drain on paper toweling; pour drippings from skillet, then measure out 2 tablespoons of drippings and return to skillet. Stir-fry onion, pepper and garlic in drippings 3 to 4 minutes, or until soft and lightly browned. Mix in parsley flakes, oregano, basil, salt, tomato sauce, wine and brown sugar and let bubble, uncovered, stirring occasionally, 5 minutes.
2. Meanwhile, toss pepperoni, chick peas and cheese together in an 8-cup baking dish. Stir in skillet mixture.
3. Bake, uncovered, in a moderate oven (375°) 1 hour, stirring casserole once or twice as it bakes.

BEEF AND EGGPLANT CASSEROLES

Make these ahead and freeze in individual packets.

Bake at 425° for 50 minutes. Makes 8 servings.

    1½ pounds ground round
      1 cup frozen chopped onion
      1 large clove garlic, minced
      2 tablespoons olive or vegetable oil
      1 envelope (1½ ounces) spaghetti sauce mix
        with mushrooms
      1 can (8 ounces) tomato sauce with cheese
      ¾ cup water
      ¾ cup dry red wine
    1½ teaspoons leaf basil, crumbled
      1 teaspoon leaf oregano, crumbled
      1 medium-large eggplant, peeled and sliced
        (about 1 pound)
      ½ cup olive or vegetable oil
      ½ cup grated Parmesan cheese (2 ounces)
      1 pound mozzarella cheese, thickly sliced

1. Brown beef with onion and garlic in 2 tablespoons oil in a large skillet. Add spaghetti sauce mix, tomato sauce, water, red wine, basil and oregano. Cover; simmer 15 minutes.

2. Sauté ½ of the eggplant slices in ¼ cup oil until limp and golden. Add remaining oil and eggplant slices. Transfer eggplant to 8 shallow oven-to-table baking dishes lined with heavy-duty foil.
3. Spoon meat sauce over eggplant. Sprinkle Parmesan cheese evenly over casseroles. Top with thick slices of mozzarella.
4. Seal packets tightly; label, date and freeze. Remove packets from casseroles; return to freezer.
5. To serve: Remove frozen block of food from foil; place in same individual baking dishes. Cover with foil. Bake in a hot oven (425°) for 50 minutes, or until sauce is bubbly-hot.

BOUNTIFUL BEAN STEW

Here's a hearty meal south-of-the-border style.

Makes 8 servings.

      1 pound dried red kidney beans
      2 quarts water
    2½ cups chopped onion (4 to 5 onions)
      6 carrots, pared and cut in ½-inch pieces
      1 can (12 ounces) tomato paste
    3½ teaspoons chili powder
      1 tablespoon salt
    1½ teaspoons garlic salt
      ¼ teaspoon pepper
      1 pound Monterey Jack cheese, cubed

1. Rinse beans in cold water. Then, cover with 2 quarts of water and bring to boiling. Boil 2 minutes. Remove from heat and let stand 1 hour. Cover, bring to boiling again; reduce heat and simmer 45 to 50 minutes, or until beans are tender.
2. Add vegetables, tomato paste and seasonings; simmer 30 to 35 minutes, or until carrots are tender. Stir cheese into hot stew just before serving.
3. If made ahead, reheat in a moderate oven (350°) about 40 minutes.

CHICKEN CORDON BLEU EN CASSEROLE

This main dish is one of those easy-to-serve foods ideal for a buffet or large sit-down dinner.

Bake at 350° for 30 minutes. Makes 8 servings.

      8 whole chicken breasts, halved, boned and
        skinned
      ⅔ cup butter
      1 teaspoon salt
      ½ teaspoon white pepper
    2⅔ cups water
      1 teaspoon salt
      4 teaspoons butter
        Pinch saffron
    2⅔ cups enriched pre-cooked rice
      3 pounds fresh broccoli, cooked
      8 slices cooked ham
    16 slices Swiss cheese (about 8 ounces)
      8 mushroom caps (optional)

1. Sauté chicken breasts in ⅔ cup butter in large frying pan until golden brown on both sides, about 30 minutes. Season with salt and pepper. Set aside, keep warm.
2. Bring water, salt, remaining 4 teaspoons butter and saffron to a boil in a medium-size saucepan. Stir in rice. Cover; remove from heat, let stand 5 minutes. Stir until fluffy.
3. Spoon rice evenly into bottom of a 3-quart shallow baking dish. Arrange reserved chicken and cooked broccoli on top; place ham slices on chicken breasts.
4. Bake in a moderate oven (350°) for 20 minutes, or until chicken is almost cooked. Add cheese slices and mushroom caps; bake 10 minutes longer, or until cheese is melted.

ITALIAN CHICKEN BAKE
This recipe makes two delicious chicken casseroles—one to eat now and one to serve on a busy day.

Bake at 350° for 30 minutes. Makes 16 servings.

  3 broiler-fryers, about 3 pounds each, cut up
  1 medium-size onion, peeled and sliced
2½ teaspoons salt
  ½ teaspoon peppercorns
  1 pound mushrooms, trimmed and sliced
  1 cup (2 sticks) butter
  1 cup fine soft bread crumbs
  ½ cup all-purpose flour
  ¼ teaspoon pepper
  ¼ teaspoon ground nutmeg
  2 cups light cream
  ½ cup dry sherry
  1 package (1 pound) thin spaghetti,
    broken in 2-inch lengths
  1 cup grated Parmesan cheese (4 ounces)

1. Combine chicken, onion, 1 teaspoon of the salt, peppercorns, and enough water to cover in a kettle. Heat to boiling; cover. Cook 40 minutes, or until chicken is tender. Remove from broth and cool until easy to handle. Strain broth into a 4-cup measure and set aside for making sauce.
2. Pull skin from chicken and take meat from bones; cube meat; place in a large bowl.
3. Sauté mushrooms in ¼ cup of the butter until soft in a large frying pan; combine with chicken.
4. Melt remaining butter in a large saucepan. Measure out ¼ cup and toss with bread crumbs in a small bowl; set aside.
5. Stir flour, remaining 1½ teaspoons salt, pepper and nutmeg into remaining butter in saucepan; cook, stirring constantly, until bubbly. Stir in 3½ cups of the chicken broth and cream. Continue cooking and stirring until sauce thickens and boils 1 minute; remove from heat. Stir in sherry.
6. While sauce cooks, cook spaghetti, following label directions; drain well. Spoon into two baking dishes, 13x9x2. Spoon chicken mixture over spaghetti; spoon sauce over all.

7. Add Parmesan cheese to bread-crumb mixture; toss lightly to mix. Sprinkle over chicken-spaghetti mixture in baking dishes.
8. Bake in moderate oven (350°) 30 minutes, or until bubbly and crumb topping is toasted. Garnish with bouquets of watercress, sliced mushrooms and pimiento strips, if you wish.
Day-before note: Fix casseroles through Step 7; cover and chill. About an hour before serving, remove from refrigerator and uncover. Bake in moderate oven (350°) 40 minutes, or until bubbly. If casseroles must stand a bit before serving, leave in oven with heat turned off.

LINGUINE ALLA MARIA TERESA
This elegant dish with a fancy name is really noodle and ham casserole, perked up with cheese and made beautiful with peppers.

Bake at 400° for 20 minutes. Makes 8 servings.

  1 package (1 pound) linguine or spaghetti
  4 cups diced cooked ham or 1 can (1 pound) ham,
    diced
  6 tablespoons (¾ stick) butter
  1 can (3 or 4 ounces) sliced or chopped
    mushrooms
  4 tablespoons all-purpose flour
  1 teaspoon salt
  1 tall can evaporated milk
  1 envelope instant chicken broth or 1 teaspoon
    granulated chicken bouillon
1⅓ cups water
  ½ cup grated Romano cheese (2 ounces)
  1 cup packaged croutons
  1 sweet red pepper
  1 green pepper
  1 tablespoon butter (for peppers)

1. Cook linguine in a kettle, following label directions; drain; return to kettle.
2. While linguine cooks, brown ham slightly in the 6 tablespoons butter in a large saucepan; remove with slotted spoon to a small bowl.
3. Drain mushroom liquid into a cup; reserve mushrooms for Step 4. Blend flour and salt into drippings in saucepan; cook, stirring constantly, just until bubbly. Stir in mushroom liquid, milk, chicken broth and water. Continue cooking and stirring until sauce thickens and bubbles 1 minute.
4. Add 2 cups of the sauce and reserved mushrooms to drained linguine; toss to mix. Spoon into a shallow 10-cup baking dish, pressing linguine up sides of dish to leave a hollow in center. Add reserved ham to remaining sauce, blending well. Spoon into hollow in pasta. Sprinkle with Romano cheese.
5. Bake in hot oven (400°) 20 minutes, or until casserole is bubbly.
6. Meanwhile, halve, seed and slice peppers; sauté in the 1 tablespoon butter until soft in small skillet.
7. Sprinkle croutons around edge of casserole; mound center with sautéed red and green peppers.

65

PORK RISOTTO

Start this pork-and-rice casserole early, for it cooks a long time.

Bake at 350° for 2 hours. Makes 8 servings.

    2 pounds lean fresh pork shoulder, cut in 1-inch
      cubes
    4 large onions, chopped (4 cups)
    2 cans (1 pound each) tomatoes
    2 cups chopped celery
    1 can (3 or 4 ounces) sliced mushrooms
    1 tablespoon sugar
    2 teaspoons salt
    1 teaspoon leaf savory
    ¼ teaspoon pepper
    1 cup uncooked rice
    2 cups grated Cheddar cheese (8 ounces)

1. Brown meat in large frying pan; remove and set aside. Sauté onions until soft in drippings in pan.
2. Stir in tomatoes, meat, celery, mushrooms and liquid, sugar, salt, savory and pepper; heat the meat mixture to boiling.
3. Layer about a third of meat mixture into a 12-cup baking dish; top with half of uncooked rice and cheese. Repeat to make a second layer of each; spoon remaining meat mixture on top; cover.
4. Bake in moderate oven (350°) 2 hours, or until pork is tender and liquid absorbed. (Add a little water during baking, if needed, to keep moist.)

DOUBLE-GOOD MANICOTTI

Half of the big noodles are stuffed with a zippy meat filling; the other half, with creamy cheese.

Bake at 350° for 40 minutes. Makes 8 servings.

    1 large onion, chopped (1 cup)
    1 clove garlic, minced
    2 tablespoons butter
    1 tablespoon Italian seasoning
    2½ teaspoons salt
    1 teaspoon sugar
    4 cans (8 ounces each) tomato sauce
    1 can (1 pound) Italian tomatoes
    1 package (12 ounces) manicotti noodles
    1 pound ground beef
    ½ cup chopped walnuts
    2 eggs
    1 package (9 ounces) frozen chopped spinach,
      thawed and drained
    1½ cups (12 ounces) cream-style cottage cheese
    3 or 4 ounces cream cheese, softened
    8 ounces sliced mozzarella or pizza cheese, cut
      in triangles

1. Sauté onion and garlic in butter just until onion is soft in a medium-size saucepan; stir in Italian seasoning, 1 teaspoon of the salt, sugar, tomato sauce and tomatoes. (Remaining 1½ teaspoons salt are for Steps 3 and 4.) Simmer sauce, stirring several times, about 15 minutes; keep hot for Step 6.
2. Cook manicotti noodles, a few at a time, in a large amount of boiling salted water, following label directions; lift out with a slotted spoon; place in a pan of cold water for Step 5.
3. Shape ground beef into a large patty in a large frying pan. Brown 5 minutes on each side, then break up into small chunks; remove from heat; cool. Stir in 1 teaspoon of the remaining salt, walnuts, 1 of the eggs and half of the spinach.
4. Blend cottage cheese, cream cheese, remaining ½ teaspoon salt, egg and spinach in a bowl.
5. Lift manicotti noodles, one at a time, from water; drain well. Fill half with meat mixture and half with cheese mixture, using a long-handle teaspoon.
6. Spoon 2 cups of the tomato-sauce mixture into a greased baking pan, 13x9x2; arrange noodles on top; spoon remaining sauce over; cover.
7. Bake in moderate oven (350°) 30 minutes; uncover. Arrange cheese triangles, overlapping, on top. Bake 10 minutes longer, or until cheese melts.

LASAGNA ROLLUPS

The filling is made from a blender-smooth combination of chicken, chicken broth and spinach.

Bake at 375° for 30 minutes. Makes 6 to 8 servings.

    1 broiler-fryer (about 2½ pounds)
    1½ cups water
    1 small onion, peeled and sliced
    1 teaspoon salt
    ¼ teaspoon pepper
    1 envelope spaghetti sauce mix
    1 can (1 pound, 12 ounces) tomato purée
      Dash of sugar
    2 tablespoons butter
    1 package (10 ounces) frozen chopped spinach,
      thawed
    ¼ teaspoon ground nutmeg
    1 package (1 pound) fluted-edge lasagna noodles
    6 ounces sliced mozzarella cheese

1. Cook chicken with water, onion, salt and pepper about 40 minutes, or until tender, in a saucepan.
2. While chicken cooks, combine spaghetti sauce mix, tomato puree, sugar and butter in a medium-size saucepan. Heat to boiling; reduce heat; cover. Simmer 30 minutes.
3. Remove chicken from broth; cool; reserve broth. Skin chicken; remove from bones, cut meat into small pieces.
4. For filling: Combine ½ cup of the reserved broth with half of the chicken and half of the spinach in an electric blender container. Whirl until smooth, about 1 minute. Place mixture in medium-size bowl, scraping sides of blender container with rubber spatula. Repeat with remaining chicken, spinach and ½ cup broth; add to mixture in bowl; add nutmeg, blending well. (If you do not have a blender, chop chicken and spinach as fine as possible, then stir in enough broth to make a smooth paste.)

5. Cook lasagna noodles in a kettle, following label directions; drain; cool in a large bowl of cold water.
6. To make rollups: Remove lasagna noodles, one at a time, from water and pat dry with toweling. Spread with scant ¼ cup chicken mixture; roll up, jelly-roll fashion. Repeat with remaining noodles.
7. Pour 2 cups of the prepared tomato sauce in the bottom of a shallow 12-cup baking dish. Arrange rollups on sauce, making two layers, if necessary. Spoon remaining sauce over rollups.
8. Bake in moderate oven (375°) 20 minutes. Cut mozzarella cheese in lengthwise strips and arrange on rollups. Bake 10 minutes longer, or until cheese is melted and sauce is bubbly-hot.

ZITI CASSEROLE
This casserole bubbles with Homemade Meat Sauce.

Bake at 350° for 40 minutes. Makes 8 servings.

1 pound ziti
2 cups (1 pound) ricotta cheese
4 ounces mozzarella cheese, diced (about 1 cup)
½ cup grated Parmesan cheese (2 ounces)
1 egg
¾ teaspoon salt
¼ teaspoon pepper
6 cups Homemade Meat Sauce (recipe follows)

1. Cook ziti and drain, following label directions.
2. While noodles are cooking, make filling: Combine ricotta, mozzarella, Parmesan, egg, salt and pepper in a large bowl.
3. Layer ziti, filling and meat sauce in a 13x9x2-inch baking dish, starting and ending with sauce.
4. Bake in moderate oven (350°) 40 minutes.

HOMEMADE MEAT SAUCE
Make a batch of this meaty home-style sauce. Use it for Ziti Casserole (recipe above). Freeze the extra.

Makes 12 cups.

1 large onion, chopped (1 cup)
2 cloves garlic, minced
¼ cup vegetable oil
1 pound ground beef
2 Italian sausages, chopped
2 cans (2 pounds, 3 ounces each) Italian tomatoes
2 cans (6 ounces each) tomato paste
2 tablespoons sugar
1 tablespoon leaf oregano, crumbled
1 tablespoon leaf basil, crumbled
1 tablespoon salt
½ teaspoon pepper
¼ cup grated Parmesan cheese (1 ounce)

1. Sauté onion and garlic in oil until soft in a large skillet; brown beef and sausage. Pour off all but 2 tablespoons fat in skillet.

2. Stir in tomatoes, tomato paste, sugar, oregano, basil, salt and pepper. Simmer, uncovered, stirring frequently, 45 minutes, or until sauce thickens. Stir in cheese; cool. Freeze in plastic containers.

SHRIMP AND NOODLES AU GRATIN
This is a snap to make with convenience foods.

Bake at 350° for 20 minutes. Makes 4 servings.

1 package noodles with sour cream and cheese sauce mix
Milk
Butter
1 package (1 pound) frozen, shelled, deveined shrimp
1 can (3 or 4 ounces) sliced mushrooms, drained
8 ounces cottage cheese
½ teaspoon dill weed
3 tablespoons fine dry bread crumbs
1 tablespoon butter, softened

1. Prepare noodles with milk and butter in a medium-size saucepan, following label directions.
2. Cook shrimp in a medium-size saucepan, following label directions; drain and chop. Add to noodles.
3. Stir in mushrooms, cottage cheese and dill weed. Spoon into a 6-cup casserole.
4. Combine bread crumbs and butter in a small bowl. Sprinkle over casserole.
5. Bake in moderate oven (350°) 20 minutes, or until casserole is bubbly-hot.

SWISS MACARONI BAKE
Swiss cheese gives this easy casserole a mild nutlike flavor. Eggs and milk make it fluffy.

Bake at 350° for 45 minutes. Makes 6 servings.

1 package (8 ounces) elbow macaroni
3 tablespoons butter
1 cup grated Swiss cheese (4 ounces)
1 cup soft bread crumbs (2 slices)
2 eggs
2 cups milk
½ teaspoon dry mustard
¼ teaspoon salt
¼ teaspoon pepper

1. Cook macaroni in boiling salted water in a kettle, following label directions; drain; spoon into an 8-cup baking dish.
2. Melt butter in a small saucepan; drizzle 2 tablespoons over hot macaroni; stir in cheese until melted. Toss bread crumbs with remaining butter in saucepan.
3. Beat eggs slightly with milk, mustard, salt and pepper in a small bowl; pour over macaroni mixture; sprinkle buttered crumbs around edge.
4. Bake in moderate oven (350°) 45 minutes, or until set and crumbs are toasty.

SOUPS

HALE AND HEARTY CHEESE SOUP
Here's a soup that makes budget-stretching a delicious pleasure!

Makes 6 main-dish servings.

    2 tablespoons butter
    ½ cup chopped celery
    2 tablespoons all-purpose flour
    3 cups milk
    2 cups peeled, cooked, diced potatoes
    1 package (10 ounces) frozen peas
    1 can (1 pound) salmon, drained, boned
        and flaked
    2 cups shredded Cheddar cheese (8 ounces)

1. Melt butter in a large saucepan; add celery and sauté until tender. Stir in flour; cook over low heat until mixture is smooth. Remove from heat.
2. Stir in milk. Heat slowly, stirring constantly, to boiling; boil 1 minute, continuing to stir.
3. Stir in potatoes, peas and salmon. Heat just until bubbly hot. Add cheese; stir until melted. Garnish with dillweed, if you wish.
Note: For a thinner soup, stir in additional milk, ½ cup at a time, to desired consistency.

SWISS POTATO SOUP
The mild flavors of cheese and potato blend so pleasingly. And this soup tastes equally delicious hot or cold.

Makes 8 servings.

    1 large onion, chopped (1 cup)
    3 tablespoons butter
    3 large potatoes, pared and cut up
    1 teaspoon salt
    ¼ teaspoon dry mustard
    ⅛ teaspoon white pepper
    3 cups water
    2 cups milk
    8 ounces sliced Swiss cheese, cut up
    2 tablespoons chopped parsley

1. Sauté onion in butter until soft in a kettle; stir in potatoes, salt, mustard, pepper and water. Heat to boiling; cover.
2. Simmer 30 minutes, or until potatoes are very soft; press through a fine sieve into a large bowl; return to kettle. Stir in milk; heat slowly just to boiling. Stir in cheese until melted.
3. Ladle into soup bowls or plates; sprinkle with parsley. Or chill several hours and serve cold.

ONION SOUP
This soup can be made ahead of time; reheat and add bread and cheese just before serving.

Makes 6 servings.

    4 large onions, sliced (1½ pounds)
    4 tablespoons (½ stick) butter
    6 cups Basic Beef Broth (recipe follows)
    2 teaspoons salt
    ¼ teaspoon pepper
    6 to 8 slices French bread, toasted
    ½ cup grated Parmesan cheese (2 ounces)
    ¼ cup grated Swiss cheese (1 ounce)

1. Sauté onion in butter in Dutch oven 15 minutes, or until lightly browned. Stir in beef broth, salt and pepper. Bring to boiling; reduce heat; cover; simmer 30 minutes.
2. Ladle soup into 6 ovenproof soup bowls or 12-ounce custard cups, or an 8-cup casserole. Lay bread slices on top, sprinkle with cheeses.
3. Heat in very hot oven (425°) 10 minutes, then place under preheated broiler until top is bubbly.

BASIC BEEF BROTH
Make this flavorful beef broth and keep on hand for making homemade soups.

Makes 14 cups.

    2½ pounds brisket, boneless chuck, or bottom
        round, in one piece
    2 pounds shin of beef with bones
    2 three-inch marrow bones
    1 veal knuckle (about 1 pound)
        Water
    8 teaspoons salt
    2 carrots, pared
    2 medium-size yellow onions, peeled
    2 stalks celery with leaves
    1 turnip, pared and quartered
    1 leek, washed well
    3 large sprigs of parsley
    12 peppercorns
    3 whole cloves
    1 bay leaf

1. Place beef, shin of beef, marrow bones and veal knuckle in a large kettle; add water to cover, about 4 quarts. Heat to boiling; skim off foam that appears on top. Add salt, carrots, onions, celery, turnip and leek; tie parsley, peppercorns, cloves and bay leaf in a small cheesecloth bag; add to kettle. Add more water if needed.
2. Heat to boiling; cover; reduce heat; simmer very slowly 3½ to 4 hours, or until meat is tender. Remove meat and vegetables from broth.
3. Strain broth through cheesecloth into a large bowl. (There should be about 14 cups.) Use this broth in the above Onion Soup or in any recipe calling for beef broth.

4. When meat is cool enough to handle, remove and discard bones. Trim meat, cut into bite-size pieces and save for a casserole, if you wish. To store in refrigerator up to 3 to 4 days, keep in covered container. To freeze, pack in small portions, 1 or 2 cups, in plastic bags or freezer containers.

5. To store broth in refrigerator, up to 4 days, leave fat layer on surface until ready to use, then lift off and discard before heating. To freeze: Transfer broth to freezer containers, allowing space on top for expansion; freeze until ready to use.

CHEESE AND OYSTER STEW
Serve this as an appetizer or main dish.

Makes 4 servings.

¼ cup (½ stick) butter
2 cups milk
2 cups light cream
½ cup finely grated Romano cheese (2 ounces)
2 tablespoons all-purpose flour
2 cans (8 ounces each) whole oysters, with juice
Salt
Finely chopped chives or green onions
Parmesan Cheese Toasts (recipe follows)

1. Heat butter with milk and cream in a large saucepan, until butter is melted.
2. Combine cheese and flour in a bowl; stir into saucepan. Stir over low heat just until mixture starts to bubble. Add oysters and juice.
3. Simmer soup 2 minutes. Stir in salt to taste. Pour into individual soup bowls; top with chives. Serve with Parmesan Cheese Toasts.

Parmesan Cheese Toasts: Lightly toast 4 slices of toasting white bread. Then spread evenly with mayonnaise or salad dressing; sprinkle lightly with grated Parmesan cheese. Cut slices in half. Place on cooky sheet and bake in moderate oven (350°) about 5 minutes, or until bubbly hot.

FRANK-AND-BEAN CHOWDER
Two favorites are made into a special family treat.

Makes 6 servings.

1 medium-size onion, chopped (½ cup)
½ pound frankfurters, sliced
2 tablespoons vegetable oil
1 cup sliced celery
1 can condensed beef broth
1 can condensed bean with bacon soup
1 can (about 1 pound) stewed tomatoes, cut up
1 can (about 1 pound) cut green beans
½ cup shredded Cheddar cheese (2 ounces)

1. Sauté onion and frankfurters in vegetable oil, stirring occasionally, until lightly browned in a large heavy saucepan or Dutch oven.

2. Add celery, beef broth, bean soup and canned vegetables with their liquids; heat just to boiling; reduce heat; cover. Simmer 5 minutes.
3. Ladle into soup plates. Sprinkle cheese over top. Serve with hot refrigerated biscuits, if you wish.

CREAMY FLORENTINE SOUP
This blender-easy soup is great for warm days, or as a light appetizer course.

Makes 8 servings.

2 packages (10 ounces each) fresh spinach
½ cup chopped shallots
3 tablespoons butter
3 cans (13¾ ounces each) chicken broth
1¼ teaspoons salt
⅛ teaspoon pepper
Dash of ground nutmeg
8 ounces cream cheese, diced

1. Trim spinach; wash leaves well; shake water off.
2. Sauté shallots in butter until soft in a large skillet. Add spinach; cover. (No need to add any water.) Cook over medium heat 10 minutes, or just until leaves are wilted.
3. Add chicken broth, salt, pepper and nutmeg; simmer 5 minutes; cool slightly.
4. Pour part of the soup at a time into container of electric blender; cover. Whirl until smooth. (Or puree through sieve or food mill.)
5. Pour into a large saucepan; add cream cheese. Heat gently, stirring constantly, just until cheese has melted into soup.
6. Pour into a bowl. Cover; chill at least 4 hours.
7. Pour into chilled serving bowl. Garnish with sieved hard-cooked egg, if you wish. Serve icy cold.

BROWN SWISS SOUP
This cousin to French onion soup makes an elegant first course with a minimum of effort.

Makes 4 servings.

¼ cup (½ stick) butter
2 cups frozen chopped onion
2 cans (13¾ ounces each) beef broth
½ cup water
2 envelopes brown gravy mix
4 thick slices French bread
Butter
1 cup shredded Swiss cheese (4 ounces)

1. Melt ¼ cup butter in a large saucepan, sauté onion until tender. Add broth and water; bring to boiling. Stir in gravy mix; simmer 5 minutes.
2. Ladle into 4 ovenproof dishes. Spread bread with butter; place one slice in each serving of soup. Divide cheese over the 4 slices of bread.
3. Place dishes in very hot oven (450°). Bake about 3 minutes, or until cheese is bubbly.

SAUCES

BASIC CHEESE SAUCE
Versatile Cheddar is the starter for three sauces.

Makes about 1½ cups.

  2 tablespoons butter
  2 tablespoons all-purpose flour
  ½ teaspoon dry mustard
  ¼ teaspoon salt
  ⅛ teaspoon seasoned pepper
  1 cup milk
  1 teaspoon Worcestershire sauce
  1 cup shredded Cheddar cheese (4 ounces)

1. Melt butter in a pan; stir in flour, mustard, salt and pepper; cook, stirring, until bubbly.
2. Stir in milk and Worcestershire sauce; continue cooking and stirring until sauce boils 1 minute. Stir in cheese until melted. Serve hot over a vegetable.

Chili-Cheese Sauce: Prepare recipe above, using ½ cup beef broth and 1 can (about 8 ounces) chili-without-beans instead of milk. Serve hot over frankfurters or hamburgers. Makes about 2 cups.

Tomato-Cheese Sauce: Prepare recipe above, using only ½ cup milk; stir in 1 can (6 ounces) tomato juice. Serve hot over sliced hard-cooked eggs on toast. Makes about 1¾ cups.

SHERRY CHEESE SAUCE
Cream cheese goes into these dress-ups for desserts.

Makes about 1⅓ cups.

  8 ounces cream cheese, softened
  ¼ cup sugar
  ¼ cup milk
  2 tablespoons cream sherry

Combine all ingredients in a small bowl; beat until well-blended; chill. Serve over strawberries.

Chocolate Velvet: Combine 8 ounces cream cheese, 5 tablespoons sugar, 1 envelope (1 ounce) liquid unsweetened chocolate, 6 tablespoons milk and ½ teaspoon vanilla in a small bowl; beat until well-blended; chill. Serve over pudding. Makes 1⅓ cups.

Lemon Cream: Combine 8 ounces cream cheese, 6 tablespoons sugar, ¼ cup milk, ¼ cup lemon juice and 1 teaspoon grated lemon rind in a small bowl; beat until well-blended; chill. Serve over warm gingerbread. Makes about 1½ cups.

CHIVE CHEESE SAUCE
This is delicious with cabbage.

Makes about 2¼ cups.

  2 tablespoons butter
  2 tablespoons all-purpose flour
  ½ teaspoon salt
  1½ cups milk
  About 6 ounces chive cream cheese

Melt butter in a medium-size saucepan; stir in flour and salt; cook, stirring constantly, until bubbly. Stir in milk; continue cooking and stirring until sauce thickens and boils 1 minute. Add cheese; stir in until melted. Serve hot over cooked cabbage.

MORNAY SAUCE
Swiss cheese seasons this classic; Parmesan goes into its variation.

Makes about 1⅓ cups.

  1 tablespoon butter
  1 tablespoon all-purpose flour
  ⅛ teaspoon white pepper
  1 small can evaporated milk (⅔ cup)
  ⅔ cup water
  1 envelope instant chicken broth
  1 egg yolk
  ½ cup shredded Swiss cheese (2 ounces)

1. Melt butter in a small saucepan; stir in flour and pepper. Cook, stirring constantly, until bubbly. Stir in milk, water and chicken broth; continue cooking and stirring until mixture boils 1 minute.
2. Beat egg yolk slightly in a small bowl; slowly beat in half of the hot mixture, then beat back into remaining mixture in pan. Cook, stirring constantly, 1 minute. (Do not boil.) Stir in cheese until melted. Serve hot over poached fish.

Parmesan Sauce: Prepare recipe above, using only ⅓ cup water and ¼ cup grated Parmesan cheese instead of Swiss. Stir in ¼ cup chopped parsley. Serve hot over baked potatoes. Makes about 1 cup.

BLUE CHEESE BUTTER
Use this to dress up an economical cut of beef.

Makes about ¾ cup.

  ½ cup blue cheese
  4 tablespoons (½ stick) butter, softened
  2 tablespoons sherry, white wine, brandy or cream

1. Crumble cheese. Allow cheese and butter to stand at room temperature 2 hours, or until soft.
2. Mash cheese with the butter in a small bowl. Use a fork first and then a spoon. Stir in sherry and mix to a smooth paste. Spoon over meats.

5
MONEY-SAVING MAIN DISHES

A little bit of cheese can go a long way toward solving a big problem —how to feed your family extravagantly well without being extravagant. With cheese, a little bit will help to stretch an economical main dish, such as pasta, into a hearty, nutritious meal. It complements economy cuts of meat, poultry and fish, too. And, since every little bit helps, you may begin to see a big, positive difference in your budget.

BEEF DINNERS

CHILI-CHEESE BEEF LOAF

Very Southwestern in flavor, this meat loaf is centered with a chili-pepper-cheese combo and topped with a bright melange of peppers and cheese.

Bake at 350° for 1 hour. Makes 8 servings.

- 1 large green pepper
- 2 pounds ground round or chuck
- ½ cup seasoned packaged bread crumbs
- 1 teaspoon salt
- ⅛ teaspoon pepper
- 1 can (8 ounces) tomato sauce
- 2 eggs
- 1 large onion, finely chopped (1 cup)
- 1 can (4 ounces) hot green chili peppers
- 5 ounces Monterey Jack cheese
- 1 jar (4 ounces) pimiento
- 2 tablespoons butter
-   Salsa Picante (recipe follows)

1. Halve pepper; seed and cut lengthwise into long strips. Chop enough to make ¼ cup; reserve remainder of the pepper for Step 7.
2. Combine beef, bread crumbs, salt, pepper, tomato sauce, eggs, onion, chopped green pepper and 1 of the canned chili peppers, chopped, in a large bowl. Mix until well blended.
3. Press half the mixture into a lightly oiled 10¼x 3⅝x2⅝-inch loaf pan. Cut pimiento into 1-inch strips; place a row of strips down center of meat.
4. Cut cheese in quarters lengthwise. Wrap 3 of the quarters with remaining chili peppers. Place wrapped cheese end-to-end on top of pimiento.
5. Press remaining meat mixture firmly over this cheese-pepper center. Unmold onto a baking pan.
6. Bake in moderate oven (350°) for 50 minutes.
7. Meanwhile, sauté remaining green pepper strips in butter 5 minutes. Arrange sautéed pepper and remaining pimiento on loaf after 50 minutes. Cut remaining quarter of cheese into long slices; arrange over peppers and pimiento. Bake loaf 10 minutes longer, or until cheese is melted. Transfer to heated serving platter. Serve with Salsa Picante.

Salsa Picante: Sauté ½ cup chopped onion in 2 tablespoons butter 10 minutes, or until tender but not brown, in a small skillet. Stir in 2 medium-size tomatoes, finely chopped (1½ cups); cook, uncovered, stirring often, over medium heat to develop flavor and evaporate some of the liquid, 5 minutes. Add ½ cup water, 1 envelope or teaspoon instant chicken broth and ¼ teaspoon crushed dried red pepper; bring to boiling; lower heat and simmer 5 minutes. Makes about 1½ cups of sauce.

Right: Hungarian Baked Chicken and Cabbage is served with apple wedges and melted cheese. The recipe is on page 83.

BLUE CHEESE BEEF LOAVES
Blue cheese tops each of these little meat loaves.

Bake at 350° for 1 hour and 15 minutes. Makes 6 servings (1 loaf each).

- 2 pounds ground beef
- 1 can (1 pound) tomatoes, well-drained
- 1 cup soft bread crumbs (2 slices)
- 1 egg, slightly beaten
- 1½ teaspoons salt
- ¼ teaspoon pepper
- 1 teaspoon Worcestershire sauce
- 2 tablespoons crumbled blue cheese

1. Combine all ingredients, except cheese; mix lightly, breaking up tomatoes, if needed. Shape into 6 individual loaves; make a small hollow in top of each for cheese. Wrap each, label, date and freeze.
2. About 1½ hours before serving time, remove loaves from freezer and unwrap; place in a pan.
3. Bake in moderate oven (350°) 1 hour; spoon 1 teaspoon blue cheese into hollow in each. Bake 15 minutes longer, or until cheese is melty.
Note: To cook loaves without freezing, bake in moderate oven (350°) 30 minutes; spoon cheese on top. Bake 10 minutes longer, or until cheese is melty and loaves are richly browned.

CHEESEBURGERS ON A STICK
The meat mixture is wrapped around a cube of cheese, so the "burger" is fastened securely to the skewer.

Makes 4 servings.

- 1 pound ground beef
- 1 egg
- ½ cup fine dry bread crumbs
- 1 envelope (1 ounce) onion burger seasoning mix
- ½ cup water
- 4 ounces Swiss cheese, cut into 24 cubes
- 6 slices bacon
- 2 medium-size peppers (1 green and 1 red), seeded and cut into cubes

1. Mix beef, egg and bread crumbs in a medium-size bowl. Combine onion burger seasoning mix and water in a 1-cup measure; add to beef mixture; toss.
2. Shape a heaping tablespoonful of beef at a time into patties in the palm of your hand; place a cheese cube in the center and shape beef around it into a ball. Chill about 1 hour, or until firm enough to hold on skewers.
3. Cut each slice of bacon in half lengthwise and then crosswise to get 4 pieces. In skillet cook about 2 minutes, or just until slightly translucent. Wrap each slice around a meatball.
4. Thread meatballs carefully, so bacon is held in place, alternating with red and green pepper cubes on 4 long skewers.
5. Broil or grill about 6 minutes per side, or until meat is done as you like it.

Left: Economy-class meat pies that don't scrimp one ounce on flavor. The selection includes Chicken Con Queso (top shelf), Beef Bourguignonne with Mock Puff Pastry (bottom left) and Ham & Cheese Deep-Dish Pie. Recipes are in this chapter.

BRONCO BUSTERS
Sauce makes enough filling for husky sandwiches plus a bonus casserole.

Makes 8 servings.

2 large onions, chopped (2 cups)
2 tablespoons butter
2 tablespoons olive or vegetable oil
2 pounds ground beef
1 package (6 ounces) sliced salami, diced
2 cans (about 1 pound each) stewed tomatoes
2 cans (6 ounces each) tomato paste
2 cups water
2 teaspoons salt
2 teaspoons sugar
1 teaspoon basil
1 teaspoon thyme
2 cans (1 pound each) red kidney beans, drained
1 teaspoon chili powder
8 long hero rolls, split, toasted and buttered
2 medium-size firm ripe tomatoes, sliced thin
  Shredded lettuce
  Shredded Cheddar cheese

1. Sauté onions in butter and olive or vegetable oil until soft in a kettle; push to one side.
2. Shape ground beef into a large patty in same kettle; brown 5 minutes on each side, then break into chunks; stir in salami; cook 3 to 4 minutes.
3. Stir in tomatoes, tomato paste, water, salt, sugar, basil and thyme; simmer 30 minutes.
4. Measure 5 cups of the sauce into a medium-size bowl; cover and set aside to make Oven Moussaka (recipe follows).
5. Stir beans and chili powder into remaining sauce in kettle; simmer 15 minutes to blend flavors.
6. Spoon about ¾ cup onto each toasted roll; top with tomato slices, shredded lettuce and cheese.

OVEN MOUSSAKA
Your freezer dividend: A hearty one-dish meal of meaty sauce, layered with browned eggplant and two kinds of cheese.

Bake at 350° for 2 hours. Makes 8 servings.

1 large eggplant
2 eggs
2 tablespoons water
½ cup fine dry bread crumbs
½ cup vegetable oil
2 cups (1 pound) cream-style cottage cheese
5 cups meat sauce (from Bronco Busters; recipe above)
1 pound (16 ounces) sliced mozzarella or pizza cheese
6 tablespoons grated Parmesan cheese

1. Pare eggplant; cut into ¼-inch-thick slices.
2. Beat 1 of the eggs slightly with water in a pie plate. Sprinkle bread crumbs on wax paper. Dip eggplant slices into egg mixture, then into crumbs.
3. Heat part of the vegetable oil in a large frying pan; add some of the eggplant slices and brown on one side; turn; cover. Steam 3 minutes, or until tender; drain on paper toweling. Repeat with remaining eggplant and oil.
4. Beat remaining egg slightly in a medium-size bowl; stir in cottage cheese.
5. Measure about 1 cup of the meat sauce into a freezer-to-oven shallow dish, 13x9x2. Cover with a third each of the cooked eggplant, cottage-cheese mixture, mozzarella and Parmesan cheeses. Repeat to make two more layers of each; spoon remaining meat sauce over top. Cover dish with foil; label, date and freeze.
6. About 2¼ hours before serving time, remove baking dish from freezer. Place, covered, in cold oven. Set temperature control at moderate (350°).
7. Bake 1¾ hours; uncover; top with additional mozzarella cheese, if you wish. Bake 15 minutes longer, or until bubbly hot in center.
Note: If baking casserole without freezing, bake, uncovered, in moderate oven (350°) for about 45 minutes, or until it's bubbly.

LAMB, PORK & VEAL

HAM AND CHEESE DEEP-DISH PIE
A mild touch of curry gives this main dish a deliciously exotic flavor. It's shown on pages 76–77.

Bake at 400° 15 minutes. Makes 6 servings.

2 cans (10¾ ounces) golden mushroom soup, undiluted
1 cup shredded Muenster cheese (4 ounces)
½ teaspoon curry powder
1 package (10 ounces) frozen mixed vegetables
3 cups diced cooked ham
1 package (8 ounces) refrigerated crescent roll dough
¼ cup (½ stick) butter, melted
¼ teaspoon garlic powder

1. Combine soup and cheese in a medium-size saucepan. Cook, stirring constantly, over low heat until cheese is melted. Remove from heat and stir in curry powder, vegetables and ham. Pour mixture while hot into a 1½-quart casserole.
2. Unroll crescent roll dough and separate into triangles. Fold each triangle in half crosswise and place end of triangle against outer edge of casserole as shown in photograph on pages 76–77. (The pie will look as if it burst open with crust turned back.) Mix butter and garlic together and brush on dough.
3. Bake casserole in hot oven (400°) 15 minutes, or until ham mixture is bubbly and crust is brown.

HAM ROLLS WITH CURRIED RICE

Flavored rice mix and packaged ham slices make a quick dinner for four.

Bake at 400° for 20 minutes. Makes 4 servings.

1 package (6 ounces) curried rice mix
2 packages (9 ounces each) frozen whole green beans
8 slices (about 1 pound) cooked ham, ⅛-inch thick
1 envelope (1½ ounces) white sauce mix
3 ounces Swiss cheese, cut up

1. Prepare rice mix following label directions; spread in a shallow 8-cup baking dish.
2. Cook green beans following label directions; drain. Divide beans among ham slices; roll up. Place rolls, seam side down, on rice in baking dish.
3. Prepare sauce mix following label directions. Add cheese; stir until melted. Pour over ham rolls.
4. Bake in a hot oven (400°) 20 minutes, or until sauce is bubbly. Sprinkle the ham rolls with chopped parsley, if you wish.

VEAL PARMIGIANA

This popular veal dish is an easy make-ahead. It may be assembled, refrigerated, then baked when you're ready for dinner.

Bake at 400° for 10 minutes. Makes 4 servings.

1 medium-size onion, chopped (½ cup)
1 clove garlic, minced
½ cup vegetable oil
1 can (1 pound, 1 ounce) Italian tomatoes
1 can (6 ounces) tomato paste
¾ teaspoon salt
2 teaspoons leaf basil, crumbled
2 teaspoons leaf oregano, crumbled
1 pound thin veal for scallopini
2 eggs, beaten
½ cup packaged bread crumbs
4 ounces sliced mozzarella cheese
¼ cup grated Parmesan cheese (1 ounce)

1. Sauté onion and garlic in 2 tablespoons of the oil until soft in a medium-size skillet. Stir in tomatoes, tomato paste, salt, basil and oregano. Simmer, uncovered, stirring frequently, 45 minutes, or until sauce thickens; reserve.
2. Place bread crumbs on wax paper. Dip veal in beaten egg, then crumbs.
3. Sauté veal, a few pieces at a time, in remaining oil, until golden brown in a large skillet; drain on paper toweling.
4. Layer half the tomato sauce, veal, remaining sauce and sliced mozzarella in a 12-inch baking dish or individual dishes.
5. Bake in hot oven (400°) 10 minutes, or until cheese is melted and sauce is bubbly-hot. Sprinkle top with Parmesan cheese.

CREAMY HAM PUFF

It's leftover ham with a cream-puff top.

Bake at 375° for 35 minutes. Makes 4 servings.

½ bunch broccoli (about ¾ pound)
2 envelopes (⅞ ounces each) white sauce mix
  Water or milk
½ cup shredded Cheddar cheese (about 2 ounces)
3 teaspoons prepared mustard with onion
½ pound cooked ham, coarsely chopped
1 large tomato, sliced
½ cup water
4 tablespoons (½ stick) butter
½ teaspoon salt
½ cup all-purpose flour
2 eggs

1. Wash and trim broccoli, cut stalks and flowerets into bite-size pieces. Cook in boiling salted water in medium-size saucepan 10 minutes, or just until crisply tender; drain.
2. While broccoli cooks, make sauce with water or milk following label directions; add cheese and mustard. Stir in ham.
3. Layer broccoli and ham mixture in a 6-cup baking dish, beginning and ending with broccoli. Arrange tomato slices on top.
4. Heat water, butter and salt to a full rolling boil in a small saucepan. Add flour all at once. Stir with a wooden spoon until mixture forms a thick smooth ball that leaves side of pan clean, about 1 minute. Remove from heat; cool slightly.
5. Beat in eggs one at a time, beating well after last addition. Spoon mixture into a pastry bag fitted with a star tip. Pipe rosettes onto tomato slices.
6. Bake in moderate oven (375°) 35 minutes, or until topping is puffed and brown and the ham is hot.

MONDAY LAMB

Try this main dish when you have leftover lamb.

Makes 6 servings.

½ cup fine dry bread crumbs
¼ cup grated Parmesan cheese (1 ounce)
½ teaspoon salt
⅛ teaspoon pepper
1 egg
1 tablespoon water
12 thin slices roast lamb
6 tablespoons (¾ stick) butter
1 lemon, cut in 6 wedges

1. Mix the bread crumbs, Parmesan cheese, salt and pepper in a pie plate.
2. Beat egg slightly with water in a second pie plate.
3. Dip lamb slices into egg mixture, then into crumb mixture to coat evenly.
4. Sauté slowly, part at a time and turning once, in butter until crusty-brown. Overlap slices on a large serving platter; serve with lemon wedges.

Next page: Roast Loin of Pork with Swiss Cheese Stuffing is surrounded by garden-fresh carrots, green beans and onions. Recipe is on page 82.

ROAST LOIN OF PORK WITH SWISS CHEESE STUFFING

The stuffing mixture is delicious with other meats, too. Try it with chicken, pork chops and fish.

Bake at 325° for 35 minutes per pound. Makes 8 servings.

    1 cup chopped red pepper
    1 cup chopped green pepper
    ⅓ cup chopped onion
    ¼ cup (½ stick) butter
    3 cups packaged herb-flavored bread stuffing
    2 tablespoons dried parsley flakes
    1 teaspoon salt
    ¼ teaspoon pepper
    1 can (1 pound) whole tomatoes
    2 cups diced Swiss cheese (8 ounces)
    5- to 7-pound pork loin (have butcher crack backbone)

1. Sauté chopped peppers and onion in butter in a large frying pan until golden brown; add stuffing mix, parsley, salt, pepper, tomatoes and cheese; blend well. (Makes about 6 cups stuffing.)
2. Cut 6 or 8 deep pockets into pork between rib bones. Fill pockets with stuffing mixture. (Any leftover stuffing may be baked separately in a covered dish during the last 30 minutes the meat roasts.)
3. Place pork loin in roasting pan. Roast in slow oven (325°) 35 minutes per pound, or until meat thermometer registers 170°F.

PIMIENTO VEAL LOAF

Serve this meat loaf with our delicious tomato-chicken broth sauce.

Bake at 350° for 1 hour. Makes 8 servings.

    2 pounds ground veal
    1 cup fine dry bread crumbs
    ½ cup grated Parmesan cheese (2 ounces)
    1 medium-size onion, chopped (½ cup)
    ¼ cup chopped pimiento-stuffed olives
    1 egg
    1½ cups tomato juice
    2 tablespoons lemon juice
    2 teaspoons salt
    ½ teaspoon pepper
    2 cans or jars (4 ounces each) whole pimientos, drained
    4 tablespoons (½ stick) butter
    ¼ cup all-purpose flour
    1 envelope instant chicken broth
    1 teaspoon salad seasoning
    1 cup water
    2 tablespoons dry sherry

1. Line a loaf pan, 9x5x3, with foil, leaving a 1-inch overhang all around; grease foil well.
2. Combine veal, bread crumbs, Parmesan cheese, onion, olives, egg, ½ cup of the tomato juice, lemon juice, salt and pepper in a large bowl; mix lightly.

3. Carefully slit each pimiento lengthwise at sides to form two pieces. Place pieces, insides up, over bottom and slightly up sides of pan. (Pimientos should cover entire bottom of pan and form a petal effect on sides.) Gently press meat mixture into pan.
4. Bake in moderate oven (350°) for about 1 hour, or until lightly brown on top.
5. Lift up on foil to loosen loaf from pan; cover pan with a heated serving platter. Turn upside down; carefully remove pan and peel off foil.
6. Melt butter in medium-size saucepan; blend in flour, chicken broth and salad seasoning. Cook, stirring constantly, until bubbly. Stir in remaining 1 cup tomato juice, water and sherry; continue cooking and stirring until sauce thickens and boils 1 minute. Slice loaf; serve with sauce.

POULTRY

SWISS-STYLE CHICKEN CUTLETS

This is one of the many variations that can be done with breaded chicken cutlets. You can vary the nuts in the breading and the cheese in the filling.

Makes 6 servings.

    6 chicken cutlets
    ¼ teaspoon salt
    ⅛ teaspoon pepper
    2 tablespoons Swiss cheese cut in ⅛-inch cubes
    2 tablespoons chopped walnuts
    2 tablespoons chopped parsley
    2 tablespoons all-purpose flour
    1 egg
    1 teaspoon each vegetable oil and water
      Salt and pepper
    ⅓ cup packaged bread crumbs mixed with 2 tablespoons finely chopped walnuts
    ¼ cup (½ stick) butter, melted

1. Cut a pocket in each cutlet. Sprinkle with salt and pepper. Mix the Swiss cheese, walnuts and parsley well, and fill each cutlet with 1 tablespoon of the mixture. Press the edges of each cutlet together.
2. Flour each cutlet. Beat the egg with the oil and water and a pinch each of salt and pepper until very liquid. Mix crumbs and nuts on piece of wax paper.
3. Brush a fine film of beaten egg on the first side of each cutlet, then invert it into the crumb and nut mixture. Brush the second side with egg also and coat with the crumb nut mixture. Pat smartly between both hands to discard excess crumbs.
4. Heat the butter in a large skillet. Panfry the cutlets until golden on both sides. It should take no longer than 8 to 10 minutes.
5. Serve with any green vegetable of your choice.

HUNGARIAN BAKED CHICKEN AND CABBAGE

Apples, caraway seed and Swiss cheese give this main dish its old-world character.

Bake at 375° for 30 minutes. Makes 4 servings.

4 tablespoons (½ stick) butter
1 whole chicken, quartered (about 3 pounds)
　Salt
　Pepper
1 small head green cabbage, cored and cut into ½-inch thick slices
1 medium-size onion, thinly sliced
2 red apples, cored and sliced
1 tablespoon grated lemon rind
2 teaspoons caraway seed
1 teaspoon sugar
2 cups shredded Swiss cheese (8 ounces)

1. Melt butter in a large skillet; brown chicken on all sides over medium heat; reduce heat, cover and cook for about 30 minutes, or until almost tender. Season with salt and pepper.
2. Place 2 cabbage slices in each of 4 (7-inch diameter) ramekins. Arrange onion and apple slices over cabbage; sprinkle with lemon rind, caraway seed and sugar. Add browned chicken to each ramekin.
3. Bake, uncovered, in moderate oven (375°) about 30 minutes, or until chicken is tender. Add cheese. Return to oven just long enough to melt cheese.

CHICKEN CON QUESO

The filling for this main-dish pie can be made in the morning and refrigerated until dinnertime. Then, heat it up while you're making the crust.

Bake at 400° for 25 minutes. Makes 6 servings.

1 chicken (about 3 pounds), cut up
　Salt and pepper
2 cans (13¾ ounces each) chicken broth
1 medium-size onion, chopped (½ cup)
1 cup sliced celery
2 carrots, sliced
⅓ cup butter
½ cup all-purpose flour
1 cup (8 ounces) heavy cream
1 cup shredded Monterey Jack cheese (4 ounces)
TOPPING:
2 cups biscuit mix
½ cup milk
3 ounces cream cheese
2 tablespoons milk
1 tablespoon chopped parsley
1 tablespoon chopped chives

1. Wash chicken pieces; pat dry. Sprinkle generously with salt and pepper. Place pieces in a large kettle or Dutch oven with cover. Add chicken broth, onion, celery and carrots. Cover; heat to boiling, then simmer 45 minutes, or until chicken is tender.
2. Remove chicken and vegetables to a 2-quart casserole. Reserve 2 cups of the broth for sauce. (Any sauce in addition to the 2 cups can be used as a base for your next pot of cheese soup.)
3. Melt butter in a saucepan over low heat; stir in flour. Gradually stir in reserved chicken broth and cream. Cook over low heat, stirring constantly, until sauce bubbles and thickens. Stir in cheese; continue cooking until cheese is melted. Season to taste with salt and pepper. Pour sauce over chicken and vegetables in casserole. Set aside while making biscuit topping. (Or, refrigerate if making early in day. Then, heat slowly, while preparing crust.)
4. Combine biscuit mix and milk in a large bowl. Remove to a lightly floured surface and knead dough a few times, or until it forms a smooth ball. Roll out to an 8-inch square.
5. Mash cream cheese with milk in a small bowl, until fluffy. Stir in parsley and chives.
6. Spread cream cheese mixture evenly over 8-inch square of dough. Roll up, jelly-roll fashion. With a sharp knife, cut roll into eight slices, each 1-inch in diameter. Place slices, side by side with cut side up, on top of casserole. Bake in a hot oven (400°) for 25 minutes, or until crust is lightly browned.

CHICKEN VALENCIA

It's baked chicken in a mouth-watering sauce.

Bake at 350° for 50 minutes. Makes 4 servings.

1 broiler-fryer (about 2½ pounds)
½ cup all-purpose flour
2 tablespoons butter
3 tablespoons vegetable oil
3 medium-size tomatoes, peeled and quartered
¼ cup pimiento-stuffed olives, sliced
1 large onion, chopped (1 cup)
1 green pepper, halved, seeded and chopped
1 teaspoon leaf basil, crumbled
1 teaspoon seasoned salt
1 teaspoon paprika
1 cup water
1 envelope or teaspoon instant chicken broth
⅓ cup grated Parmesan cheese
2 large oranges, pared and sectioned

1. Cut chicken into serving-size pieces. Shake chicken, a few pieces at a time, in a plastic bag with flour; tap off excess. Reserve 1 tablespoon of the flour.
2. Sauté chicken in butter and oil, turning once, 15 minutes, or until golden brown, in a skillet. Place in a 10-cup baking dish. Add tomatoes and olives.
3. Add onion and green pepper to drippings in skillet; sauté until tender. Stir in basil, the 1 tablespoon reserved flour, seasoned salt and paprika. Cook 1 minute, stirring constantly. Stir in water and chicken broth; cook and stir until sauce thickens and bubbles 1 minute. Stir in cheese and orange sections. Pour over chicken and vegetables; cover.
4. Bake in moderate oven (350°) for about 50 minutes, until the chicken is tender.

Next page: Cheese and Oyster Stew is served with Parmesan Cheese Toasts, a green salad and—as a main attraction—Baked Stuffed Red Snapper. Recipe for snapper is on page 86. See Chapter 4 for soup and toast recipes.

FISH

BAKED STUFFED RED SNAPPER
The stuffing for this dish is so incredibly easy to make, you'll want to try it with almost any white-meat fish.

Bake at 350° for 45 minutes. Makes 4 to 6 servings.

¼ cup finely chopped parsley
¼ cup (½ stick) butter
2 cups plain croutons
1 cup (8 ounces) cottage cheese with spring vegetables
1 egg, slightly beaten
½ teaspoon salt
1 red snapper (or any white-meat fish), about 3½ pounds, cleaned and scaled
⅓ cup melted butter
Juice of 1 lemon
½ teaspoon salt

1. Sauté parsley in ¼ cup butter in a large frying pan, 1 minute. Remove from heat and stir in croutons, cottage cheese, egg and salt.
2. Stuff body cavity of fish with cheese-egg mixture. Sew or skewer the opening to keep filling inside.
3. Combine melted butter, lemon juice and salt in a pan. Line a shallow baking pan with foil and brush the foil with some of the butter mixture. Brush remaining butter mixture over fish.
4. Bake fish in a moderate oven (350°) for 45 minutes, or until fish flakes easily. Garnish with clusters of watercress and sautéed fluted mushroom caps. Serve with an appetizer course of Cheese and Oyster Stew (recipe is on page 69), and with a salad with oil and vinegar dressing.

FLOUNDER FILLETS WITH CHEESE SAUCE
Here's high protein packed into an easy-to-make main dish special.

Bake at 350° for 30 minutes. Makes 8 servings.

2 packages (10 ounces each) frozen broccoli spears
2 pounds frozen flounder fillets, thawed
¼ cup (½ stick) butter
3 cups milk
1½ teaspoons salt
¼ teaspoon pepper
2 cups shredded Swiss cheese (about 6 to 8 ounces)

1. Cook broccoli, following label directions; drain well. Arrange in a 12-cup shallow baking dish. Cut flounder fillets into serving-size pieces, if necessary. Fold the fillets and place on top of the broccoli.

2. Melt butter in a saucepan; sauté onion until tender. Stir in flour; cook, stirring constantly, until bubbly. Add milk. Cook over medium heat, stirring constantly, until sauce thickens and bubbles. Stir in salt, pepper and cheese; continue stirring until cheese melts. Pour over fish.
3. Bake in moderate oven (350°) 30 minutes, or just until fish flakes easily with a fork. Sprinkle lightly with paprika, if you wish.

LOBSTER THERMIDOR
Lobster meat subtly seasoned is served beautifully in the shell.

Bake at 425° for 15 minutes. Makes 4 servings.

2 small live lobsters, weighing about 1¼ pounds each
5 tablespoons butter
4 tablespoons all-purpose flour
½ teaspoon paprika
½ teaspoon dry mustard
¼ teaspoon salt
Dash of cayenne
1 cup light cream
1 can (3 or 4 ounces) chopped mushrooms, drained
2 tablespoons dry sherry
¼ cup unsalted soda-cracker crumbs
¼ cup grated Parmesan cheese (1 ounce)

1. Drop live lobsters into a very large kettle of rapidly boiling salted water; cover. Cook over high heat 8 to 10 minutes. Lobsters will turn a bright red. Remove at once with tongs; drain; let cool long enough to handle.
2. Remove meat from each lobster, saving shells for restuffing, this way: Place lobster on its back; twist off the two large claws, then crack claws and remove meat; set aside.
3. Cut lobster down middle from head to tail with scissors, then cut through hard shell of back and the thin membrane on either side of tail. Lift out the pink coral (roe), if any, and green tomalley (liver); dice and set aside for filling in Step 4. Discard stomach sac or "lady" from back of head, black vein running from head to tail, and spongy gray tissue. Lift out all meat; dice. Set the lobster shells on a large cooky sheet.
4. Sauté lobster meat in 4 tablespoons of the butter in a medium-size frying pan 2 minutes; stir in flour, paprika, mustard, salt and cayenne; cook, stirring constantly, until bubbly. Stir in cream; continue cooking and stirring until mixture thickens and boils 1 minute; remove from heat. Stir in mushrooms, tomalley, coral and sherry. (Mixture will be very thick.) Spoon into lobster shells.
5. Melt remaining 1 tablespoon butter in a small saucepan; add cracker crumbs and cheese; toss lightly to mix. Sprinkle over filling in shells.
6. Bake in hot oven (425°) 15 minutes, or until filling is hot and crumb topping is golden color.

MEATLESS MAIN DISHES

KANSAS CORN SCALLOP
This main dish gets its name from 2 kinds of corn.

Bake at 325° for 1 hour. Makes 6 servings.

- **1 can (12 or 16 ounces) whole-kernel corn**
- **2 eggs**
- **1 can (1 pound) cream-style corn**
- **1 small can evaporated milk (⅔ cup)**
- **4 tablespoons (½ stick) butter, melted**
- **2 tablespoons instant minced onion**
- **½ teaspoon salt**
- **¼ teaspoon pepper**
- **2 cups coarsely crushed saltines**
- **12 ounces Swiss cheese, diced**

1. Drain liquid from whole-kernel corn into a cup.
2. Beat eggs slightly in a large bowl; stir in corn and ¼ cup of the liquid, cream-style corn, evaporated milk, melted butter, onion, salt and pepper; fold in saltines and diced cheese. Spoon into a greased 8-cup baking dish.
3. Bake in slow oven (325°) 1 hour, or until set. Let stand 5 minutes before serving.

CLASSIC WELSH RAREBIT
This dish makes a superb light supper.

Makes 4 servings.

- **1 cup beer**
- **1 teaspoon dry mustard**
- **2 teaspoons Worcestershire sauce**
- **Few drops liquid red-pepper seasoning**
- **1 pound Cheddar cheese, shredded (4 cups)**
- **2 eggs**
- **1 tablespoon cornstarch**
- **8 slices toast or 4 English muffins**

1. Combine beer, mustard, Worcestershire sauce and red-pepper seasoning in the top of a double boiler; warm over simmering water.
2. Stir in cheese, part at a time, until melted.
3. Beat eggs and cornstarch slightly in a small bowl; slowly stir in about 1 cup of the hot cheese mixture; stir back into remaining cheese in double boiler. Cook, stirring, 3 minutes; remove from heat.
4. Halve each slice of toast diagonally, or halve English muffins; place 4 triangles of toast or 2 English muffin halves on each serving plate; spoon cheese mixture over top. Salt to taste and sprinkle with paprika, if you wish. Serve hot.

TOMATO-CHEESE TART
It's a tart brimming with Cheddar cheese.

Bake at 325° for 20 minutes. Makes 4 servings.

- **½ package piecrust mix**
- **1 cup shredded Cheddar cheese (4 ounces)**
- **3 cups shredded Swiss cheese (12 ounces)**
- **3 ripe medium-size tomatoes**
- **1 teaspoon salt**
- **1 teaspoon leaf basil, crumbled**
- **1 teaspoon leaf oregano, crumbled**
- **⅛ teaspoon pepper**
- **½ cup chopped green onions**
- **2 tablespoons butter**
- **2 tablespoons soft bread crumbs**

1. Prepare piecrust mix, following label directions, adding ½ cup of the Cheddar cheese. Roll out to a 12-inch round on a lightly floured pastry board; fit into a 9-inch pie plate. Trim overhang to ½ inch; turn under; flute to make a stand-up edge. Prick well with fork.
2. Bake in hot oven (425°) 10 to 15 minutes, or until golden; cool.
3. Spoon remaining Cheddar cheese and Swiss into piecrust. Slice tomatoes in half lengthwise and then into thin wedges. Arrange, slightly overlapping, in an attractive circular pattern over the cheese. Sprinkle with salt, pepper, basil and oregano.
4. Sauté green onions in butter until tender in a small skillet. Spoon in the center of pie; sprinkle with bread crumbs.
5. Bake in moderate oven (325°) 20 minutes, or until tomatoes are tender.

PASTA

CHEDDAR CHEESE SAUCE

Makes about 2½ cups.

- **4 tablespoons (½ stick) butter**
- **¼ cup all-purpose flour**
- **¼ teaspoon salt**
- **Dash of pepper**
- **2½ cups milk**
- **1 teaspoon Worcestershire sauce**
- **2 cups shredded Cheddar cheese (8 ounces)**

Melt butter in a medium-size saucepan. Blend in flour, salt and pepper; cook, stirring constantly, just until bubbly. Stir in milk; continue cooking and stirring until sauce thickens and bubbles 1 minute. Stir in cheese and Worcestershire sauce until cheese is melted. Use in manicotti recipe on page 89.

MANICOTTI ALLA VENEZIANA
This can be made early in the day and refrigerated. Then, about 45 minutes before serving time, warm in moderate oven (350°) 30 minutes..

Makes 6 to 8 servings.

  1 package (8 ounces) manicotti noodles
  1 pound meat-loaf mixture
  1 large onion, chopped (1 cup)
  1 clove garlic, minced
  1 cup fresh bread crumbs (2 slices)
  1 egg, beaten
½ cup chopped parsley
  1 teaspoon leaf basil, crumbled
  1 teaspoon salt
    Dash of pepper
    Cheddar Cheese Sauce (recipe on page 87)

1. Cook manicotti noodles, a few at a time, following label directions; lift out carefully with a slotted spoon; place in a large bowl of cold water.
2. Shape meat-loaf mixture into a large patty in a large skillet; brown 5 minutes on each side, then break up into small pieces; remove with a slotted spoon to a medium-size bowl.
3. Sauté onion and garlic until soft in drippings in skillet. Add to cooked meat with bread crumbs, egg, parsley, basil, salt and pepper, mixing well.
4. Lift manicotti noodles from water, one at a time; drain well. Fill each with part of the meat mixture.
5. Pour half the hot Cheddar Cheese Sauce into the bottom of a shallow 12-cup flameproof dish. Place manicotti over sauce. Top with remaining sauce.
6. Broil, 4 inches from heat, 5 minutes, or until golden and bubbly.

PASTA WITH PINE NUTS AND RAISINS
You can make this delightful pasta dish in minutes.

Makes 6 servings.

  1 can (1 pound) Italian tomatoes
¼ cup olive or vegetable oil
¾ cup raisins
¾ cup pine nuts
½ teaspoon salt
¼ teaspoon freshly ground pepper
  1 package (1 pound) fusilli (spiral spaghetti)
    or 1 package (1 pound) thin spaghetti
¼ cup (½ stick) butter
  1 cup grated Parmesan cheese (4 ounces)

1. Heat tomatoes and oil in a small saucepan for 10 minutes, breaking up the tomatoes with the back of a spoon. Add raisins, pine nuts, salt and pepper. Simmer while cooking pasta.
2. Cook fusilli or spaghetti, following label directions; drain well. Return to kettle and toss with butter until evenly coated. Add tomato mixture and Parmesan cheese and toss until evenly coated.
3. Turn onto heated serving platter and serve.

PINWHEEL GNOCCHI
Tender green spinach and fluffy potatoes pinwheel together to make this potato version of a classic Italian favorite.

Bake at 400° for 25 minutes. Makes 4 servings.

  1 package (10½ ounces) frozen chopped spinach
  1 cup (8 ounces) ricotta cheese
  1 cup grated Parmesan cheese (about 4 ounces)
¼ teaspoon ground nutmeg
¼ teaspoon salt
¼ teaspoon pepper
  2 pounds potatoes, pared
  2 eggs, beaten
  3 cups sifted all-purpose flour
  2 tablespoons butter, melted

1. Cook spinach following label directions; squeeze and press all water out of spinach; spread on paper toweling. Chop very fine.
2. Combine spinach, ricotta, ½ cup of the Parmesan cheese, nutmeg, salt and pepper in a small bowl. Refrigerate until ready to use.
3. Cook potatoes in boiling salted water until tender in a large saucepan; drain; toss over very low heat 2 minutes to dry potatoes.
4. Mash potatoes until smooth in a large bowl; beat in eggs. Blend in 2¾ cups of the flour to make a soft dough. Knead on lightly floured pastry board, adding only enough flour to keep dough from sticking. Roll out to a 14-inch square; spread with filling; roll up, jelly-roll fashion. Wrap in plastic wrap; refrigerate at least 1 hour.
5. Carefully cut into 1-inch slices. Place, overlapping, in a 9x9x2-inch greased baking pan. Spoon melted butter over the top and sprinkle with remaining Parmesan cheese.
6. Bake in hot oven (400°) 25 minutes, or until top of casserole is golden-brown.

GENOESE CHEESE SAUCE
This creamy sauce, delicately spiked with garlic, is good on spaghetti or noodles.

Makes enough for 4 servings, or 8 ounces of spaghetti or noodles.

½ cup chopped parsley
¼ clove garlic, minced, or dash of garlic powder
  3 tablespoons grated Parmesan cheese
  3 tablespoons olive or vegetable oil
¼ teaspoon salt
  3 or 4 ounces cream cheese, softened
½ cup light cream

1. Combine parsley, garlic or garlic powder, Parmesan, oil and salt in a small bowl. Stir in softened cream cheese and cream; mix until well blended.
2. Spoon sauce over drained hot spaghetti or noodles in a heated serving dish; toss lightly to coat well. Serve immediately.

Left: Classic Welsh Rarebit is a blending of cheese, beer and peppy seasonings. The recipe for this satisfying main dish is on page 87.

PASTA CON CINQUE FORMAGGI

Try a new pasta shape and toss it with five special cheeses.

Makes 6 servings.

- **1 package (1 pound) mostaccioli, ziti, rigati or elbow macaroni**
- **¼ cup (½ stick) butter or margarine**
- **1 cup shredded Swiss cheese (4 ounces)**
- **1 cup shredded Bel Paese cheese (4 ounces)**
- **1 cup shredded mozzarella cheese (4 ounces)**
- **1 cup shredded Provolone cheese (4 ounces)**
- **1 cup heavy cream**
- **¼ teaspoon pepper**
- **¼ cup grated Parmesan cheese**

1. Cook and drain pasta in a large kettle, following label directions, and keeping 1 cup cooking liquid in kettle; return pasta to kettle.
2. Toss pasta with butter or margarine, Swiss cheese, Bel Paese, mozzarella, Provolone, heavy cream and pepper over low heat, until cheeses melt evenly and coat pasta. Spoon into a heated dish; sprinkle with Parmesan cheese and serve.

FETTUCINI ALFREDO

Toss homemade noodles with butter and cheese.

Makes 4 servings.

- **3 cups sifted all-purpose flour**
- **2 teaspoons salt**
- **3 eggs**
- **3 tablespoons olive or vegetable oil**
- **¼ cup cold water**
  Cornstarch
- **½ cup (1 stick) butter, cut in small pieces**
- **2 cups grated Parmesan cheese (8 ounces)**
  Freshly ground black pepper

1. Sift flour and salt into a large bowl; make a well in center; add eggs, oil and water. Work liquids into flour with fingers to make a stiff dough.
2. Turn dough out onto a large pastry board. (Do not add additional flour.) Knead 10 minutes, or until dough is as smooth and soft as perfectly kneaded bread dough. Wrap dough in plastic wrap and allow to rest at room temperature 1 hour.
3. Sprinkle pastry board with cornstarch. Roll out dough, a quarter at a time, to a rectangle so thin you can read the cover of FAMILY CIRCLE through it.
4. Fold dough into quarters lengthwise. Slice dough across into ¼-inch-wide strips. Unwind strips and allow to dry on clean towels for 1 hour. Repeat with remaining quarters of dough.
5. Heat 6 quarts of water to boiling in a large kettle; add 2 tablespoons salt and 1 tablespoon oil. Cook fettucini 5 minutes. Drain and place on a platter.
6. Add pieces of butter and toss with fork and spoon until butter melts. Add Parmesan cheese and continue to toss until fettucini are coated and glistening. Grind black pepper over the top.

FARFALLE LEONARDO

Tiny egg-noodle bows are tossed with a quick, yet rich, tomato sauce for super family eating.

Makes 4 servings.

- **1 pound bulk sausage**
- **1 large onion, chopped (1 cup)**
- **1 clove garlic, minced**
- **1 can (1 pound) tomatoes**
- **1 teaspoon leaf oregano, crumbled**
- **1 teaspoon leaf basil, crumbled**
- **1 teaspoon salt**
- **⅛ teaspoon pepper**
- **1 package (8 ounces) farfalle**
- **½ cup grated Parmesan cheese**

1. Flatten sausage meat into a large patty in a large skillet. Brown on one side; turn and brown on second side. Remove sausage from skillet and crumble onto paper towels.
2. Drain off all but 2 tablespoons of fat in skillet. Sauté onion and garlic in skillet until soft. Drain tomatoes; reserve liquid. Brown tomatoes in same skillet for 5 minutes. (This is an Italian cooking trick for a tomato sauce with special flavor.)
3. Return crumbled sausage to skillet with liquid from canned tomatoes, oregano, basil, salt and pepper. Simmer, stirring occasionally, 30 minutes.
4. Cook farfalle, following label directions, until done as you like pasta. Drain and place on large heated serving platter. Spoon sauce over and top with Parmesan cheese. Toss at the table and serve.

SPAGHETTI CARBONARA

Try bacon and eggs this favorite Italian style and discover a double-quick supper dish.

Makes 6 servings.

- **1 pound spaghetti**
- **½ pound sliced bacon, diced**
- **1 large green pepper, halved, seeded and diced**
- **3 eggs**
- **½ teaspoon leaf marjoram, crumbled**
- **½ teaspoon salt**
  Dash of pepper
- **4 tablespoons (½ stick) butter**
- **1 cup grated Romano cheese (4 ounces)**

1. Cook spaghetti in boiling salted water, following label directions; drain and place on heated platter.
2. While pasta cooks, fry bacon until crisp in a skillet. Remove with a slotted spoon to paper toweling. Drain off all but 2 tablespoons bacon fat from skillet. Sauté green pepper in skillet until soft.
3. Beat eggs in a small bowl. Stir in marjoram, salt and pepper.
4. Toss butter with hot spaghetti until melted. Add seasoned eggs and toss until completely blended. Add bacon, green pepper and grated cheese. Toss once more and serve at once.

6
CHEESE & EGGS

In this chapter, two naturally compatible foods team up to bring you irresistible dishes that are nutritious and economical. There are recipes for omelets, soufflés and quiches, as well as other cheese-and-egg combinations you'll like. Tips for making the soufflés and omelets are included, and they illustrate how really simple it is to make these classics. Whip them up whenever the spirit moves you!

OMELETS

DOUBLE CHEESE OMELET
Tender cheese-filled omelet is a luncheon delight.

Makes 2 servings.

  1 cup vegetable-salad creamed cottage cheese
  1 teaspoon instant minced onion
  4 eggs
½ teaspoon salt
    Dash of pepper
  1 tablespoon butter
¼ cup shredded Cheddar cheese (1 ounce)

1. Combine cottage cheese with onion in a small bowl. Reserve.
2. Beat the 4 eggs slightly with salt and pepper in a small mixing bowl.
3. Heat a 10-inch skillet for 5 seconds. With a fork, swirl butter over bottom and sides of skillet.
4. Pour in egg mixture. Cook, stirring with flat of fork and shaking pan back and forth until omelet is firm on bottom but still slightly soft on top. Remove skillet from heat.
5. Sprinkle omelet with Cheddar cheese; spoon cottage cheese mixture down center. Fold over one third of omelet; roll omelet onto heated platter.

OMELET SECRETS
A perfect omelet is pure gold—never brown—light and delicate in texture, soft and voluptuous in the center. To make an omelet you'll need fresh eggs, good-quality butter, a bit of practice, the right pan and a generous dash of self-confidence. In addition, keep these tips in mind:
1. Allow eggs to sit at room temperature about an hour before preparing the omelet.
2. Do not overbeat the eggs or they will become thin, and the omelet will be tough.
3. Use a heavy cast-aluminum skillet that's rounded where the sides meet the bottom. Heat the skillet until thoroughly hot. To test: Flick on a few drops of water. When they dance about, skillet is ready.
4. Butter skillet right up to the rim, using about 1 tablespoon butter. As butter foams, pour in the eggs. Do not allow butter to brown before adding the omelet mixture, or it will change the color of the omelet and, furthermore, may tend to make it stick to the skillet.
5. Keep pan on medium heat with heat readily adjustable.
6. Omelets should always be served at once on warm, not hot, plates or they will go on cooking.

PUFFY OMELET WITH CHEESE SAUCE
The green chili and Swiss cheese sauce makes a nice change of pace—and stretches the food budget.

Bake at 350° for 10 minutes. Makes 2 servings.

  4 tablespoons (½ stick) butter
  2 tablespoons all-purpose flour
¾ teaspoon salt
  1 cup milk
  1 cup shredded Swiss cheese (4 ounces)
  4 eggs, separated
  2 tablespoons water
    Dash of pepper
  1 tablespoon chopped green chili (from a 4-ounce can)

1. Make cheese sauce: Melt 2 tablespoons of the butter in a small saucepan; add flour and ½ teaspoon of the salt. Cook over low heat, stirring constantly, just until bubbly. Remove from heat; stir in milk slowly. Cook, stirring constantly, until sauce thickens and bubbles 1 minute. Remove from heat; stir in cheese little by little until melted and smooth. Cover; keep warm while preparing remaining ingredients.
2. Beat egg whites until stiff in a large bowl. Heat oven to moderate (350°).
3. Beat egg yolks with remaining ¼ teaspoon salt and pepper until thick and lemon-colored in a small bowl; beat in water. Fold into egg white mixture until no streaks of yellow remain.
4. Heat a 9-inch skillet or omelet pan with an oven-proof handle, 5 seconds over medium heat. With a fork, swirl remaining 2 tablespoons butter over bottom and sides.
5. Pour in egg mixture. Cook over low heat 5 minutes, or until mixture is set on the bottom and is golden-brown. Then bake in preheated oven 10 minutes, or until puffy and lightly golden on top.
6. Loosen omelet around edge with a knife; lift onto heated large serving plate. Cut a gash with a knife down center of omelet; sprinkle green chili over one half. Spoon about ¾ cup of the cheese sauce over omelet; fold over with a wide spatula. Spoon remaining sauce over the top. Serve at once.

ITALIAN FRITTATA
Here's an easy-cheesy Italian omelet that doesn't need turning.

Makes 4 servings.

½ cup chopped green pepper
  1 medium-size onion, chopped (½ cup)
  4 tablespoons (½ stick) butter
  1 large tomato, peeled and chopped
  1 teaspoon salt
¼ teaspoon leaf oregano, crumbled
  8 eggs
⅛ teaspoon pepper
½ cup shredded provolone cheese (2 ounces)

1. Sauté green pepper and onion in 2 tablespoons of the butter until soft, about 5 minutes, in a small skillet. Add tomato, ½ teaspoon of the salt and oregano. Cook slowly, 10 minutes, stirring occasionally, until all liquid is absorbed; reserve.

2. Beat eggs slightly in a medium-size bowl with remaining ½ teaspoon salt and pepper.

3. Heat a 10-inch skillet for 5 seconds. With a fork, swirl the remaining 2 tablespoons butter over bottom and sides of pan.

4. Pour in egg mixture. Cook, stirring with flat of fork and shaking pan back and forth until omelet is firm on bottom and almost set on top. Spread tomato mixture evenly over top. Sprinkle with cheese; cover skillet for about 2 minutes, or until cheese starts to melt. Cut in wedges to serve.

CRÊPES

SHRIMP CRÊPES A LA MORNAY
Make-ahead crêpes are filled with cheese-wine-shrimp sauce that will delight discriminating palates.

Makes 12 servings.

CRÊPES:
- 1¼ cups sifted all-purpose flour
- 2 tablespoons sugar
- ½ teaspoon salt
- 3 eggs
- 3 cups milk
- 4 tablespoons (½ stick) butter, melted

FILLING:
- 6 tablespoons (¾ stick) butter
- ¼ cup chopped green pepper
- 6 tablespoons all-purpose flour
- ¼ teaspoon salt
- 2 cups milk
- ¼ cup dry white wine
- ¾ cup shredded Swiss cheese (3 ounces)
- 1 pound cooked, shelled, deveined shrimp

1. Sift 1¼ cups flour, sugar and ½ teaspoon salt onto wax paper. Beat eggs until light in a medium-size bowl; add dry ingredients; blend until smooth. Stir in 3 cups milk to make a thin batter.

2. Cover; let stand at room temperature 1 hour.

3. Heat a large heavy skillet or a Swedish pancake pan over low heat. Test temperature by sprinkling on a few drops of water; when drops bounce about, temperature is right. Lightly grease pan with butter.

4. Use 2 to 3 tablespoons of batter for each crêpe; bake until top appears dry and underside is golden; turn, lightly brown other side. Repeat, lightly greasing skillet before each baking. You will have about 24 crêpes when you're finished.

5. Place on heated serving platter and keep warm while making the filling.

6. To make crêpe filling: Melt butter in a large-size saucepan; sauté green pepper until golden brown. Remove from heat and stir in 6 tablespoons flour and ¼ teaspoon salt until mixture forms a smooth paste. Gradually stir in 2 cups milk; return to heat and cook, stirring constantly, over medium heat until sauce thickens. Cook 1 minute longer.

7. Add wine and cheese. Cook, stirring constantly, over medium heat just until cheese melts. Add shrimp; continue cooking until shrimp are thoroughly heated. Fill crêpes with shrimp mixture and spoon extra sauce on top.

CHEESE BLINTZES
Serve this treat as a main dish or dessert.

Makes 12 servings.

BATTER:
- 5 eggs
- 2 cups sifted all-purpose flour
- 2½ cups milk
- ⅓ cup vegetable oil
- Cheese Filling:
- 4 cups (2-pound carton) cream-style cottage cheese
- 2 eggs
- ⅓ cup sugar
- 1½ teaspoons vanilla
- ⅓ cup butter

TOPPING:
- 1 can (1 pound, 5 ounces) cherry pie filling
- 2 cups (16-ounce carton) dairy sour cream

1. Beat eggs just until blended in a large bowl; sift flour over the eggs and beat in just until smooth; stir in milk and oil. Cover; chill for at least 45 minutes. While batter chills, prepare filling.

2. To make Cheese Filling: Combine cottage cheese, eggs, sugar and vanilla in large bowl. Beat at high speed with electric beater 3 minutes, or until smooth.

3. Heat a heavy 8-inch skillet slowly; test temperature by sprinkling on a few drops of water. When drops bounce about, temperature is right. Grease skillet lightly with part of the butter.

4. Measure batter, a scant ¼ cup at a time, into skillet, tilting it to cover the bottom completely.

5. Cook blintz 1 to 2 minutes, or until top is set and underside is golden; remove to a plate. Repeat with remaining batter to make 24 blintzes. Sandwich each blintz with a piece of foil or wax paper to keep separated.

6. Place 3 tablespoons of the cheese filling down the center of the browned side of each blintz. Overlap two opposite sides over filling, then fold up ends toward middle on seam side.

7. Melt remaining butter in a large skillet. Brown blintzes, seam side down, turning to brown on other side. Keep warm until all blintzes have been browned. Serve blintzes warm, topped with cherry pie filling and a dollop of sour cream.

CANNELLONI
Tender pancakes are the start for this delicious dish.

Bake at 350° for 20 minutes. Makes 8 servings.

- **1 pound chicken livers**
- **5 tablespoons butter**
- **1 large onion, chopped (1 cup)**
- **1 clove garlic, crushed**
- **½ pound ground beef**
- **1 teaspoon salt**
- **¼ teaspoon fennel seed, crushed**
- **¼ teaspoon leaf sage, crumbled**
- **¼ teaspoon leaf thyme, crumbled**
- **¾ cup grated Parmesan cheese (3 ounces)**
- **1 recipe Basic Crêpes (recipe follows)**
- **3 tablespoons all-purpose flour**
- **¼ teaspoon ground nutmeg**
- **1½ cups milk**

1. Sauté livers in 2 tablespoons of the butter until brown, in a skillet, 5 minutes. Remove; mince.
2. Sauté onion and garlic until tender, about 5 minutes, in same skillet; add ground beef and brown thoroughly. Return chicken livers to pan; add salt, herbs and ¼ cup of the Parmesan cheese.
3. Make and bake 8 Basic Crêpes; keep warm.
4. Melt remaining 3 tablespoons butter in a small saucepan; stir in flour and nutmeg. Cook until bubbly. Stir in milk; cook and stir until thickened.
5. Spoon about ¼ cup of meat filling into each crêpe; roll up. Place, seam side down, in a single layer in a shallow 13x9x2-inch baking dish. Spoon sauce over crêpes; sprinkle with remaining cheese.
6. Bake in moderate oven (350°) 20 minutes, or until sauce is lightly browned.

BASIC CRÊPES

Makes 8 eight-inch crêpes.

- **¾ cup sifted all-purpose flour**
- **1 tablespoon sugar**
- **½ teaspoon salt**
- **3 eggs**
- **1 cup milk**
- **2 tablespoons butter, melted**

1. Sift flour, sugar and salt onto wax paper.
2. Beat eggs just until blended in a large bowl; add flour mixture and beat just until smooth; stir in milk and 1 tablespoon of the melted butter.
3. Heat an 8-inch heavy skillet; test temperature by sprinkling on a few drops of water. When drops bounce about, temperature is right. Grease lightly with part of remaining butter.
4. Measure batter, a scant ⅓ cup at a time, into pan, tilting pan to cover bottom completely.
5. Cook 1 to 2 minutes, or until tops are set and undersides are golden; turn. Cook 1 to 2 minutes longer, or until bottoms brown. Repeat with remaining batter, greasing skillet each time.

SEAFOOD-STUFFED CRÊPES
Thin-thin pancakes rolled around a crunchy salmon-tuna filling bake in a creamy sauce.

Bake at 350° for 30 minutes. Makes 8 servings.

FILLING AND SAUCE:
- **1 can (about 8 ounces) salmon, drained, boned, and flaked**
- **1 can (about 7 ounces) tuna, drained and flaked**
- **1 can (5 ounces) water chestnuts, drained and chopped or ½ cup finely diced celery**
- **1 tablespoon minced onion**
- **5 tablespoons butter**
- **⅓ cup all-purpose flour**
- **1 teaspoon salt**
- **⅛ teaspoon pepper**
- **2 cups milk**
- **4 tablespoons grated Parmesan cheese**
- **1 tablespoon lemon juice**

CRÊPES:
- **¾ cup all-purpose flour**
- **1 tablespoon sugar**
- **½ teaspoon salt**
- **3 eggs**
- **1 cup milk**
- **1 tablespoon melted butter**

TOPPING:
- **¼ cup heavy cream**

1. Make filling and sauce: Mix salmon, tuna and water chestnuts or celery in a medium-size bowl.
2. Sauté onion in butter just until soft in a medium-size saucepan. Blend in flour, salt and pepper; cook, stirring all the time, just until mixture bubbles. Stir in milk; continue cooking and stirring until sauce thickens and boils 1 minute. Remove from heat; blend in 2 tablespoons of the cheese and lemon juice. (Save remaining cheese for Step 8.)
3. Stir 1 cup sauce into tuna-salmon mixture; set remaining aside for Step 8.
4. Make crêpes: Measure flour, sugar and salt into sifter. Beat eggs until thick in a medium-size bowl; sift dry ingredients over; beat just until smooth. Stir in milk and butter.
5. Heat an 8-inch heavy frying pan slowly; test temperature by sprinkling in a few drops of water. When drops bounce about, temperature is right. Grease pan with butter.
6. Pour batter, a scant ⅓ cup at a time, into pan, tilting pan to cover bottom completely. Bake 1 to 2 minutes, or until top is set and underside golden; turn; brown other side. Repeat procedure, lightly buttering pan before each baking, to make 8 crêpes.
7. Spoon about ⅓ cup filling into center of each crêpe as it's baked; roll up and place, seam side down, in a shallow baking dish.
8. Make topping: Beat cream until stiff in a small bowl; fold into remaining sauce from Step 3; spoon over crêpes. Sprinkle with remaining cheese.
9. Bake in moderate oven (350°) 30 minutes, or until filling is hot and cheese is golden. Garnish with parsley, if you wish.

BEEF CRÊPES CONTINENTAL
These light-as-a-feather pancakes are filled with a scrumptious beef-cheese combination.

Bake at 375° for 20 minutes. Makes 6 servings.

       Basic Crêpes (see recipe on page 94)
   5 tablespoons butter
   3 tablespoons all-purpose flour
   1 teaspoon salt
   ¼ teaspoon pepper
   2 cups milk
   ½ cup light cream
   1 cup grated Parmesan cheese (4 ounces)
   1 medium-size onion, chopped (½ cup)
1½ pounds ground beef
   1 can (3 or 4 ounces) chopped mushrooms

1. Following recipe for Basic Crêpes on page 94, make 12 crêpes, using 7-inch frying pan; set aside while making sauce and filling.
2. Melt 4 tablespoons of the butter in a medium-size saucepan; blend in flour, ½ teaspoon of the salt and ⅛ teaspoon of the pepper. Cook, stirring constantly, until bubbly. Stir in milk and cream; continue cooking and stirring until sauce thickens and boils 1 minute; remove from heat. Stir in ¾ cup of the Parmesan cheese; keep warm.
3. Sauté onion in remaining 1 tablespoon butter until soft in a large frying pan; push to one side.
4. Shape ground beef into a large patty; place in same pan. Brown 5 minutes on each side, then break up into chunks. Stir in ½ cup of the cheese sauce, mushrooms and liquid, remaining ½ teaspoon salt and ⅛ teaspoon pepper.
5. Spoon 2 tablespoonfuls of the meat filling onto each baked crêpe; roll up tightly, jelly-roll fashion. Place in a baking pan, 13x9x2; spoon remaining sauce over top. Sprinkle with the remaining cheese.
6. Bake in a moderate oven (375°) 20 minutes.

SOUFFLÉS

HAM SOUFFLÉ
Here's a great way to use up leftover ham.

Bake at 350° for 45 minutes. Makes 6 servings.

¼ cup (½ stick) butter
¼ cup all-purpose flour
½ teaspoon dry mustard
¼ teaspoon salt
   1 cup milk
¼ cup grated Parmesan cheese (1 ounce)
   1 cup ground cooked ham
   6 eggs, separated

1. Melt butter in a medium-size saucepan; stir in flour, mustard and salt; cook, stirring constantly, just until bubbly. Stir in milk; continue cooking and stirring until sauce bubbles 1 minute.
2. Stir in cheese and ham; cool while beating eggs.
3. Beat egg whites just until they form soft peaks in a large bowl. Beat egg yolks until creamy-thick in a second large bowl; blend in cooled sauce. Stir in about 1 cup of the beaten egg whites until blended, then fold in remainder until no streaks of white remain. Pour into an ungreased 8-cup soufflé or straight-side baking dish. Gently cut a deep circle in mixture about 1 inch from edge with a rubber spatula.. (This gives soufflé its double-puffed top.)
4. Bake in moderate oven (350°) 45 minutes, or until puffy-firm and golden on top. Serve at once.

BAKED SPINACH AND EGGS AU GRATIN
Here's a high protein meal that will also be high on your list of favorites!

Bake at 325° for 45 minutes. Makes 4 servings.

   2 cups bread cubes (6 slices)
   ½ cup (1 stick) butter
   2 packages (10 ounces each) frozen chopped spinach
   1 medium-size onion, chopped (½ cup)
   4 ounces Muenster cheese, diced (about 1 cup)
   2 teaspoons salt
   ⅛ teaspoon pepper
   ⅛ teaspoon ground nutmeg
   ¼ cup all-purpose flour
   1 cup milk
   ⅓ cup grated Parmesan cheese
   8 eggs

1. Sauté bread cubes in 2 tablespoons of the butter in medium-size skillet until golden; place in the bottom of a lightly greased 6-cup baking dish. Sauté onion until tender in same skillet in 2 more tablespoons butter; reserve.
2. Cook spinach, following label directions, in medium-size saucepan; drain very well. Return to saucepan; add onion, Muenster cheese, salt, pepper and nutmeg. Spoon over bread cubes.
3. Melt remaining butter in a small saucepan; stir in flour; cook, stirring constantly, just until mixture bubbles. Stir in milk slowly; continue cooking and stirring until sauce thickens and bubbles 1 minute. Remove from heat.
4. Stir in Parmesan cheese. Let mixture cool.
5. Separate 4 of the eggs. Beat egg whites in a medium-size bowl just until they form soft peaks.
6. Beat egg yolks in a large bowl until thick and fluffy; beat in cooled white sauce mixture, a small amount at a time. Carefully fold in egg whites until no streaks of white remain.
7. Make 4 indentations with a spoon in the spinach mixture, 1 inch from edge of dish. Carefully break remaining eggs, one in each indentation. Spoon soufflé mixture completely over top, right to edge.
8. Bake in moderate oven (325°) 45 minutes.

TRIPLE CHEESE SOUFFLÉ

This recipe offers a great way to use up bits and pieces of leftover cheese. Use any favorite hard cheese, such as Cheddar or Swiss.

Bake at 325° for 1 hour and 15 minutes. Makes 6 to 8 servings.

1½ cups shredded cheese (6 ounces)
 6 tablespoons (¾ stick) butter
 ⅓ cup all-purpose flour
 1 teaspoon salt
 1 teaspoon onion powder
1½ cups milk
   Few drops liquid red-pepper seasoning
 3 eggs, separated

1. Prepare an ungreased 6-cup soufflé or straight-side baking dish this way: Fold a piece of foil, 28 inches long, in half lengthwise; wrap around dish to make a 3-inch stand-up collar; hold in place with string and a paper clip.
2. Use any combination of cheeses you have in your refrigerator, to make the 1½ cups. (We used Cheddar, Muenster and Parmesan.)
3. Melt butter in a medium-size saucepan; stir in flour, salt and onion powder; cook, stirring constantly, until mixture bubbles 1 minute; stir in milk and red-pepper seasoning; continue cooking and stirring until mixture thickens and bubbles 1 minute; stir in grated cheeses until melted; let cool while beating eggs.
4. Beat egg whites till they form soft peaks in bowl.
5. Beat egg yolks well in small bowl; beat in cooled cheese sauce very slowly until well blended. Fold this mixture into beaten egg whites until no streaks of white or yellow remain. Pour into prepared dish; make a deep circle in center with knife so soufflé will puff up high.
6. Bake in slow oven (325°) for 1 hour, 15 minutes, or until puffy-firm and golden. Serve at once.

SOUFFLÉ TIPS YOU SHOULD KNOW

1. Separate eggs as soon as you remove them from the refrigerator. It's easier to separate them when they're cold.
2. Separate the eggs carefully. The tiniest speck of yolk in whites will keep them from beating to their lightest.
3. Allow egg whites to sit at room temperature a while before beating them; then beat just until they form soft peaks that stand, then bend over when beater is raised.
4. Make sauce and let cool while beating eggs.
5. Use a wire whip to fold in beaten whites gently, just until no streaks of white or yellow remain.
6. Choose the right size ungreased soufflé or baking dish with straight sides.
7. Leave a baked soufflé in the oven for time given in the recipe, then test this way: Shake the dish gently; if center is firm, it should be done.

SOUFFLÉED BROCCOLI ROULADE

This is a puffy mixture rolled jelly-roll fashion.

Bake at 325° for 45 minutes. Makes 6 servings.

 4 tablespoons (½ stick) butter
 ½ cup sifted all-purpose flour
 ½ teaspoon salt
 2 cups milk
 4 eggs, separated
 2 packages frozen broccoli
 ¾ cup shredded Swiss cheese (3 ounces)
   Swiss Cheese Sauce (recipe follows)

1. Grease a 15x10x1-inch jelly-roll pan; line with wax paper; grease paper; dust with flour.
2. Melt butter in a medium-size saucepan. Off heat, blend in flour and salt; stir in milk. Cook, stirring constantly, until mixture is very thick.
3. Beat egg whites until they form soft peaks in a medium-size bowl. Beat egg yolks slightly in a large bowl. Slowly beat hot mixture into egg yolks, until blended. Fold beaten egg whites into egg yolks until no streaks of yellow remain. Spread in pan.
4. Bake in moderate oven (325°) 45 minutes, or until golden and top springs back when touched.
5. While omelet roll bakes, cook broccoli, following label directions; drain, cut into 1-inch pieces. Reserve ½ cup for garnish.
6. Make Swiss Cheese Sauce (see recipe below).
7. Remove omelet roll from pan this way: Loosen around edges with spatula; cover with wax paper or foil. Place a large cooky sheet or tray on top, then quickly turn upside down. Lift pan; peel paper.
8. Arrange broccoli in a single layer on top of roll; sprinkle with cheese and drizzle ½ cup hot cheese sauce over. Starting at a 10-inch end, roll up omelet, jelly-roll fashion, lifting wax paper or foil as you roll to steady and guide it.
9. Lift roll onto a heated large serving platter with two wide spatulas. Drizzle about ½ cup more sauce over roll and garnish with reserved broccoli.
10. Cut roll into thick slices. Pass remaining sauce.

SWISS CHEESE SAUCE

Makes 2½ cups.

 ⅓ cup butter
 ⅓ cup all-purpose flour
 ½ teaspoon salt
 ⅛ teaspoon pepper
 2 cups milk
 ¾ cup shredded Swiss cheese (3 ounces)

1. Melt butter over low heat in a medium-size saucepan. Stir in flour, salt and pepper; cook, stirring constantly, just until mixture bubbles.
2. Stir in milk; continue cooking and stirring until sauce thickens and bubbles 1 minute; stir in cheese until melted. Keep warm. Serve with Souffléed Broccoli Roulade (recipe above).

CHEESE SOUFFLÉ WITH EGGS AND SAUCE FLORENTINE

Hard-cooked eggs add something extra special to this light, fluffy soufflé.

Bake at 350° for 45 minutes. Makes 6 to 8 servings.

2 packages (9 ounces each) frozen creamed spinach
4 hard-cooked eggs, peeled and halved
1 small onion, chopped (¼ cup)
¼ cup (½ stick) butter
¼ cup all-purpose flour
½ teaspoon salt
½ teaspoon dry mustard
1 cup milk
 Few drops liquid red-pepper seasoning
4 eggs, separated
1 cup shredded Swiss or Muenster cheese (4 ounces)

1. Heat spinach following package directions; pour into greased 6-cup soufflé or straight-side baking dish. Arrange cut surfaces of eggs against side of the soufflé or baking dish.
2. Sauté onion until soft in butter in small heavy saucepan. Blend in flour, salt and mustard; cook, stirring constantly, just until bubbly.
3. Stir in milk and red-pepper seasoning; continue cooking and stirring, until sauce thickens and bubbles 1 minute. Remove from heat. Sauce will be thick. Beat egg yolks into sauce, one at a time, beating well after each addition.
4. Beat egg whites just until they form soft peaks in a large bowl. Stir about one-fourth of egg whites into sauce; stir in cheese; fold into remaining egg whites. Carefully pour on top of spinach in dish.
5. Bake in moderate oven (350°) 45 minutes, or until puffed and golden brown. Serve at once.

BAKED SALMON AND GREEN BEAN PUFF

Salmon and green beans, aromatic with dill, bake under a cloud of cheese soufflé. It's a casserole so showy no one will guess it's quick and easy.

Bake at 375° for 50 minutes. Makes 4 servings.

1 package (9 ounces) frozen green beans
2 tablespoons water
1 can (1 pound) salmon
1 can condensed Cheddar cheese soup
2 tablespoons all-purpose flour
1 tablespoon grated Parmesan cheese
½ teaspoon dillweed
1 tablespoon spicy brown prepared mustard
1 tablespoon minced drained capers
1 tablespoon caper juice
⅛ teaspoon pepper
SOUFFLÉ TOPPING:
4 eggs, separated
¼ teaspoon salt
¼ teaspoon dillweed
 Pinch of pepper
2 tablespoons grated Parmesan cheese

1. Cook beans in water in a small covered saucepan over moderate heat, about 5 minutes until tender but still crisp.
2. Meanwhile, drain and flake the salmon, discarding any large bones or pieces of skin. Blend ¼ cup of the soup with the flour, then combine with the remaining soup; mix in grated Parmesan, dillweed, mustard, minced capers, caper juice and the ⅛ teaspoon of pepper.
3. Drain beans well and place in an 8-cup soufflé dish. Add salmon and cheese soup mixture; stir well to mix. Bake, uncovered, in a moderate oven (375°) for 20 minutes.
4. When casserole has baked almost 20 minutes, prepare Soufflé Topping. Beat egg whites with salt to soft peaks; beat yolks with dillweed and pepper until smooth, then stir in grated Parmesan. Spoon a little beaten whites into yolk mixture; then pour yolks over whites and fold in gently until no streaks of white or yellow show. Spoon quickly on top of hot beans and salmon, return to oven and bake 30 minutes longer until puffy and touched with brown. Rush to the table and serve.

QUEEN'S CHEESE SOUFFLÉ

Cream and cottage cheeses, sparked with snips of chives and parsley, make this double-puff beauty.

Bake at 350° for 45 minutes. Makes 6 to 8 delicious servings.

3 tablespoons butter
3 tablespoons all-purpose flour
1 teaspoon salt
1 cup milk
 Few drops liquid red-pepper seasoning
3 or 4 ounces cream cheese, softened
½ cup cream-style cottage cheese
1 tablespoon chopped parsley
1 teaspoon finely cut chives or 1 teaspoon freeze-dried chopped chives
6 eggs, separated

1. Melt butter in a medium-size saucepan; stir in flour and salt; cook, stirring constantly, just until bubbly. Stir in milk and red-pepper seasoning; continue cooking and stirring until sauce thickens and boils for about 1 minute.
2. Beat in cream and cottage cheeses, then stir in parsley and chives; remove from heat; let the mixture cool while you're beating eggs.
3. Beat egg whites just until they form soft peaks in a large bowl.
4. Beat egg yolks until creamy-thick in a second large bowl; blend in cooled cheese sauce; fold in beaten egg whites until no streaks of white remain. Pour into an ungreased 8-cup soufflé or straight-side baking dish; gently cut a deep circle in mixture about 1 inch in from edge with a rubber spatula. (This gives soufflé its double-puffed top.)
5. Bake in moderate oven (350°) 45 minutes, or until puffy-firm and golden on top. Serve at once.

GOLDEN CHEESE SOUFFLÉ

This specialty, easily made with Muenster and bacon bits, looks like a masterpiece.

Bake at 350° for 45 minutes. Makes 6 servings.

6 slices bacon, diced
3 tablespoons all-purpose flour
½ teaspoon salt
½ teaspoon dry mustard
1 cup milk
   Few drops liquid red-pepper seasoning
1 cup shredded Muenster cheese (4 ounces)
6 eggs, separated
¼ cup chopped parsley

1. Sauté bacon until crisp in a small heavy saucepan; remove with a slotted spoon and drain on paper toweling. Pour off all drippings, then measure 3 tablespoonfuls and return to pan.
2. Blend in flour, salt and mustard; cook, stirring constantly, just until bubbly.
3. Stir in milk and red-pepper seasoning; continue cooking and stirring until sauce thickens and boils 1 minute. Stir in cheese until melted; remove from heat. Let mixture cool while beating eggs.
4. Beat egg whites just until they form soft peaks in a medium-size bowl. Beat egg yolks until creamy-thick in a large bowl; blend in cooled cheese sauce, bacon and parsley; fold in beaten egg whites until no streaks of white remain. Pour into an ungreased 8-cup soufflé or straight-side baking dish.
5. Bake in moderate oven (350°) 45 minutes. or until puffy-firm and golden-brown on top. Serve.

LOBSTER-RICE SOUFFLÉ

It puffs high and handsome—and stays there—without any sleight of hand.

Bake at 325° for 1 hour. Makes 6 servings.

¼ cup raw rice
¼ teaspoon salt (for rice)
¾ cup boiling water
4 eggs
4 tablespoons (½ stick) butter
4 tablespoons all-purpose flour
½ teaspoon salt (for sauce)
1 cup milk
1 can (6 ounces) lobster meat, drained, boned and cut into bite-size pieces
   Swiss-Cheese Sauce (recipe follows)

1. Stir rice and ¼ teaspoon salt into boiling water in small saucepan; cover; simmer 20 minutes, or until rice is tender and water is absorbed.
2. Separate eggs, putting whites into medium-size bowl, yolks into large bowl.
3. Melt butter over low heat in medium-size saucepan. Stir in flour and ½ teaspoon salt; cook, stirring all the time, just until mixture bubbles. Stir in milk slowly; continue cooking and stirring until sauce is very thick and boils one minute; remove from heat.
4. Beat egg whites just until they form soft peaks.
5. Beat egg yolks well; slowly stir in cream sauce, cooked rice and lobster. Lightly fold in beaten egg whites until no streaks of sauce or egg white remain. Pour into ungreased 8-cup deep baking dish.
6. Set dish in baking pan on oven shelf; pour in boiling water to depth of 1 inch.
7. Bake in slow oven (325°) 1 hour, or until top is firm and puffy-golden. Serve at once with Swiss-Cheese Sauce.

Swiss-Cheese Sauce: Melt 2 tablespoons butter over low heat in medium-size saucepan. Stir in 2 tablespoons all-purpose flour, ½ teaspoon salt and ½ teaspoon dry mustard, then cook, stirring all the time, just until mixture bubbles. Stir in 1½ cups milk slowly; continue cooking and stirring until sauce thickens and boils 1 minute. Stir in 1 cup (4 ounces) freshly grated Swiss cheese until melted. Makes 2 cups.

HERBED CHEESE SOUFFLÉ

This is excellent party fare. The single-serving soufflés are frozen in advance and popped into the oven just before your guests arrive.

Bake at 350° for 45 minutes. Makes 6 servings.

2 tablespoons finely chopped shallots or green onions
6 tablespoons (¾ stick) butter
6 tablespoons all-purpose flour
1 teaspoon salt
1½ cups milk
½ teaspoon Dijon-style mustard
   Few drops liquid red-pepper seasoning
1 cup shredded Swiss cheese (4 ounces)
6 eggs, separated
2 tablespoons chopped parsley
¼ teaspoon leaf tarragon, crumbled
¼ teaspoon leaf marjoram, crumbled

1. Butter six 1-cup soufflé dishes or 10-ounce straight-side custard cups.
2. Sauté shallots in butter until tender in medium-size saucepan about 5 minutes. Stir in flour and salt; cook, stirring constantly, until mixture bubbles. Gradually stir in milk. Continue cooking and stirring until mixture thickens and bubbles 1 minute. Stir in mustard, red-pepper seasoning and cheese. Remove from heat.
3. Beat egg yolks well in small bowl; beat into hot cheese sauce. Stir in parsley, tarragon and marjoram.
4. Beat egg whites until stiff in large bowl. Fold in yolk mixture until no streaks of white or yellow remain. Pour into prepared dishes, dividing evenly. Cover with transparent wrap. Freeze.
5. To Bake: Place frozen soufflés on cooky sheet for easy handling. Bake in moderate oven (350°) 45 minutes, or until puffed and golden. Serve with crusty bread and tomato salad, if you wish.

Left: Quiche Lorraine is a deceptively simple-to-make appetizer or main dish. Recipe is on page 104.

Next page: Light and creamy Shrimp Crêpes A La Mornay. Recipe is on page 93.

DOUBLE-BOILER CHEESE SOUFFLÉ

This puffed-up tempter stays up even if serving time is delayed a bit. Reheats perfectly, too, in its same double-boiler cooker.

Makes 4 servings.

- **2 tablespoons butter**
- **2 tablespoons all-purpose flour**
- **½ teaspoon dry mustard**
- **½ teaspoon salt**
- **1 cup milk**
- **1 cup grated Swiss cheese (4 ounces)**
- **4 eggs, separated**

1. Melt butter in a medium-size saucepan; stir in flour, mustard and salt; cook, stirring all the time, just until mixture bubbles. Stir in milk slowly; continue cooking and stirring until sauce thickens and boils 1 minute.
2. Stir in cheese until melted. Remove from heat; let cool while beating eggs.
3. Beat egg whites just until they form soft peaks in a medium-size bowl.
4. Beat egg yolks well in a large bowl; beat in cooled cheese sauce *very slowly*; fold in beaten egg whites until no streaks of white or yellow remain. Pour into top of 8-cup double boiler with cover.
5. Cook, covered, over gently boiling water, 1 hour, or until a knife inserted in center comes out clean.

DOUBLE CHOICE SOUFFLÉ

Your family has a choice in this soufflé—ham, spinach or both—in a well-seasoned cheese mixture.

Bake 300° for 1 hour and 15 minutes. Makes 4 generous-size servings.

- **6 tablespoons (¾ stick) butter**
- **6 tablespoons all-purpose flour**
- **½ teaspoon salt**
- **¼ teaspoon dry mustard**
- **⅛ teaspoon pepper**
- **½ teaspoon onion salt**
- **1½ cups milk**
- **1 cup shredded Cheddar cheese (4 ounces)**
- **6 eggs, separated**
- **½ cup finely chopped cooked ham**
- **½ cup well-drained cooked spinach, finely chopped**

1. Prepare an ungreased 5-cup soufflé or straight-side baking dish this way: Fold a piece of foil 2 inches longer than outside measurement of dish in half lengthwise; wrap around dish to make 3-inch stand-up collar. Hold foil in place with string and paper clip. Take a second piece of foil, about 12 inches long, and fold in half crosswise. Reserve.
2. Melt butter in a medium-size saucepan; stir in flour, salt, dry mustard, pepper and onion salt; cook, stirring constantly, just until mixture bubbles. Stir in milk slowly; continue cooking and stirring until sauce bubbles 1 minute. Remove from heat.

Right: Cheese Soufflé with Eggs and Sauce Florentine combines three totally compatible foods—cheese, eggs and spinach. The recipe is on page 97.

3. Stir in cheese, just until melted; let the mixture cool while you're beating the eggs.
4. Beat egg whites in a medium-size bowl just until they form soft peaks.
5. Beat egg yolks in a large bowl until thick and fluffy; beat in cooled cheese mixture, a small amount at a time, until blended. Measure out one cup of mixture into a medium-size bowl; stir in ham. Stir spinach into mixture remaining in the other bowl. Beat about ¼ cup of egg white into each bowl to loosen up mixture. Carefully fold in remaining egg whites, dividing evenly between both bowls, until no streaks of white remain.
6. Holding the 6-inch piece of foil in place in the center of the prepared soufflé dish, carefully spoon the ham mixture into one side of the dish and the spinach mixture on the other side. Slowly and carefully pull the piece of foil out.
7. Bake in slow oven (300°) 1 hour and 15 minutes, or until puffy-firm and golden. Serve at once.

QUICHE

SHRIMP CHEESE SQUARES

A deep-sea version of popular Quiche Lorraine.

Bake at 450° for 15 minutes, then at 350° for 15 minutes. Makes 35 squares.

- **1 package piecrust mix**
- **1 cup chopped green onions**
- **1 tablespoon butter**
- **2 cups shredded Swiss cheese (8 ounces)**
- **1 package (1 pound) frozen, shelled, deveined shrimp, cooked**
- **8 eggs**
- **4 cups light cream**
- **2 teaspoons salt**
- **⅛ teaspoon pepper**
- **⅛ teaspoon cayenne**

1. Prepare piecrust mix, following label directions, or make double-crust pastry recipe. Roll out, half at a time, to 9x6-inch rectangle; fit both halves into 15½x10½x1-inch jelly-roll pan. Seal together edges of halves. Prick with fork.
2. Bake in hot oven (425°) 5 minutes; remove to wire rack; cool slightly. Increase oven to 450°.
3. Sauté green onions in butter till soft, in skillet, 5 minutes. Sprinkle cheese evenly in a layer in pastry shell; add onions and shrimp.
4. Beat eggs slightly in a large bowl; slowly beat in cream, salt, pepper and cayenne; pour into shell.
5. Bake in hot oven (450°) for 15 minutes; lower heat to 350°. Bake 15 minutes more, or until the center of the quiche is almost set.

CREAMY CHEDDAR VEGETABLE SAUCE

This is an all-purpose kind of sauce you can serve over broccoli, green beans, asparagus, mushrooms, cauliflower or eggplant.

Makes about 3½ cups.

  **1 cup sliced fresh mushrooms or 1 can
    (4 ounces) sliced mushrooms, drained
  2 tablespoons butter
  3 tablespoons regular all-purpose flour
  ¼ teaspoon salt
  1 cup milk
  1 cup dairy sour cream
  2 cups grated sharp Cheddar cheese (8 ounces)
  1 tablespoon Worcestershire sauce
  1 teaspoon dry mustard**

1. Melt butter in a medium-size saucepan over low heat; sauté mushrooms 2 to 3 minutes. Stir in flour and salt. Remove from heat; gradually stir in milk. Return to medium heat; cook, stirring constantly, until sauce thickens. Cook 2 minutes longer.
2. Fold in sour cream, cheese, Worcestershire sauce and dry mustard. Cook over medium heat just until cheese melts and sauce is heated. Pour into sauceboat, or directly over a favorite vegetable.

CREAMY NOODLES ROMA

Served as a side dish with veal, this is delicous!

Makes 4 servings.

  **½ package medium-size noodles
  1 package white sauce mix
  1 tablespoon butter
  ⅓ cup grated Parmesan cheese**

1. Cook noddles, following label directions. Drain. Return to saucepan.
2. Prepare white sauce, following label directions. Stir in butter and cheese. Pour over noodles; toss.
3. Arrange on platter with veal. Sprinkle with additional cheese, if you wish.

CHEESY ITALIAN GREEN BEANS

Fresh tomato slices topped with melting cheese add extra zest to this oven-easy green bean bake.

Bake at 325° for 30 minutes. Makes 6 servings at 58 calories each.

  **1 envelope or teaspoon instant onion broth
  ½ cup boiling water
  1 package (9 ounces) frozen Italian green beans
  3 tomatoes, peeled and sliced
  1 teaspoon instant minced onion
  ½ teaspoon salt
  1 teaspoon leaf oregano, crumbled
  2 ounces part-skim mozzarella cheese, shredded
    (about 4 tablespoons)**

1. Dissolve onion broth in boiling water; add green beans. Cook 3 minutes.
2. Turn beans and liquid into shallow 6-cup baking dish. Top with tomato slices; sprinkle with minced onion, salt, oregano and cheese.
3. Bake in slow oven (325°) 30 minutes, or until beans are bubbly and cheese is melted.

SWISS POTATO SCALLOP

Mild Swiss cheese bakes melty-smooth between the layers of potatoes.

Bake at 325° for 2 hours. Makes 6 servings.

  **6 medium-size potatoes, pared and sliced thin
  6 ounces Swiss cheese, grated (about 1½ cups)
  1½ teaspoons salt
  ¼ teaspoon pepper
  1 cup heavy cream or 1 cup evaporated milk
  1 tablespoon grated onion
    Paprika**

1. Layer ⅓ of the potatoes into a baking dish, 13x9x2; sprinkle with ⅓ each of the cheese, salt and pepper. Repeat with remaining potatoes, cheese and seasonings to make two more layers of each.
2. Combine cream or evaporated milk and onion in a 1-cup measure; pour over layers. Sprinkle with paprika; cover.
3. Bake in slow oven (325°) 2 hours, or until potatoes are tender and liquid is absorbed.

CHEDDAR-STUFFED EGGPLANT

The stuffing is delicious and versatile. Try it sometime with squash, instead of the eggplant.

Bake at 350° for 30 minutes. Makes 8 servings.

  **2 medium-size eggplants
  ½ cup chopped onion
  ½ cup chopped green pepper
  2 tablespoons butter
  2 medium-size ripe tomatoes, peeled and chopped
  1 teaspoon salt
  ½ teaspoon pepper
  1 cup grated sharp Cheddar cheese (4 ounces)
  ⅔ cup bread crumbs**

1. Cut eggplants in half lengthwise and carefully scoop out interior, leaving a ¼-inch shell. Cube the scooped-out portion; reserve.
2. Sauté onion and green pepper in butter in a large frying pan, just until golden. Add chopped tomatoes, salt, pepper and the reserved cubed eggplant; sauté just until tender. Add cheese and ⅓ cup of the bread crumbs; mix just until blended.
3. Spoon the cheese-bread-crumb mixture into eggplant shells; place in greased baking pan. Sprinkle the remaining ⅓ cup crumbs over stuffing.
4. Bake in moderate oven (350°) for 30 minutes, or until eggplant is tender. Serve immediately.

Left: A fresh vegetable selection that includes broccoli with Creamy Cheddar Vegetable Sauce. The recipe is on this page.

Next page: Cheddar-Stuffed Eggplant is an easy bake-in-the-oven choice. Recipe is on this page.

FRENCH ONION SCALLOP

Dunk the crisp big bread cubes into this rich-with-cheese onion dish. Wonderful eating!

Bake at 350° for 30 minutes. Makes 6 servings.

    6 large onions, sliced
    4 tablespoons (½ stick) butter
    4 tablespoons all-purpose flour
    ½ teaspoon salt
    ¼ teaspoon pepper
    2 cups milk
    1 teaspoon Worcestershire sauce
    6 slices Swiss cheese, cut in pieces
    6 slices buttered slightly dry French bread, cubed

1. Cook sliced onions in boiling water to cover in large saucepan 10 to 12 minutes, or just until tender but still firm; drain well. Arrange in buttered shallow 6-cup baking dish.
2. While onions cook, melt butter in medium-size saucepan; remove from heat. Blend in flour, salt and pepper; slowly stir in milk and Worcestershire.
3. Cook, stirring constantly, until sauce thickens and boils 1 minute. Stir in cheese, keeping over low heat until melted.
4. Pour over onions; stir to mix; arrange bread cubes around edge.
5. Bake in moderate oven (350°) 30 minutes, or until bread is golden.

SPRING BROCCOLI PLATTER

An onion-cheese sauce and slices of French bread give this dish its unique flavor.

Makes 6 servings.

    1 bunch broccoli (about 2 pounds)
    2 tablespoons butter
    1 Bermuda onion, chopped
    2 tablespoons all-purpose flour
    ½ teaspoon salt
    ⅛ teaspoon pepper
    1½ cups milk
    ½ pound Cheddar cheese, cut up
    ¼ cup mayonnaise or salad dressing
    12 thin slices French bread, toasted

1. Cut coarse leaves from broccoli stems; if stems are thick, split lengthwise and pare; cook in about 1-inch depth boiling salted water in saucepan 12 to 15 minutes, or just until tender; drain carefully.
2. While broccoli cooks, melt butter in saucepan; add chopped onion; sauté slowly, stirring often, just until tender; remove from heat; blend in flour, salt and pepper; slowly stir in milk.
3. Cook, stirring constantly, until sauce thickens and boils 1 minute; stir in and melt cheese; fold in mayonnaise or salad dressing.
4. Arrange broccoli with stems at center on heated round platter; stand toast between broccoli stems to form a circle; spoon hot sauce into center.

Right: Stuffed Artichoke Parmesan offers delicious eating as an appetizer course or with a main dish. Recipe is on this page.

POTATO GNOCCHI

Dumplings, Northern Italian style, tender and cheesy.

Bake at 400° for 15 minutes. Makes 8 servings.

    2 pounds potatoes, pared
    2 eggs, beaten
    1 teaspoon salt
    3 cups sifted all-purpose flour
    1 can condensed chicken broth
    8 cups water
    ½ cup (1 stick) butter, melted
    1 cup grated Parmesan cheese

1. Cook potatoes in boiling salted water until tender in a large saucepan; drain and toss over very low heat 2 minutes to dry potatoes.
2. Mash potatoes until smooth in a large bowl; beat in eggs and salt. Blend in flour to make a soft dough. Cover bowl and chill at least 1 hour.
3. Heat chicken broth and water to boiling in a large kettle. Drop dough by teaspoonfuls, a few at a time, into boiling liquid and simmer 5 minutes, or until slightly puffed. Remove with a slotted spoon to a shallow baking dish.
4. Drizzle with butter and sprinkle with cheese.
5. Bake in hot oven (400°) 15 minutes, or until puffy and golden. Serve at once.

STUFFED ARTICHOKE PARMESAN

As you can see by the photograph on the next page, this is a scrumptious looking vegetable dish. What's more, it tastes delicious too.

Makes 4 servings.

    2 cups coarse white bread crumbs
    ½ cup chopped parsley
    ½ cup grated Parmesan cheese (2 ounces)
    1 tablespoon chopped onion
    1 clove garlic, finely chopped
    ¾ teaspoon salt
    ⅛ teaspoon pepper
    4 large artichokes
    4 tablespoons olive or vegetable oil
    Melted butter
    Lemon slices

1. Combine crumbs, parsley, cheese, onion, garlic, salt and pepper in a medium-size bowl; toss lightly.
2. Cut stems from artichokes close to base; slice about an inch from top with a sharp knife and snip off any spiny leaf tips. Carefully spread leaves open; remove small inner yellow leaves. Scrape out fuzzy chokes with teaspoon. Rinse artichokes in water.
3. Spoon stuffing mixture into center hollow of each artichoke; stand in deep kettle. Pour 1 tablespoon olive oil over each; pour boiling water into kettle to a depth of 2 inches. Heat to boiling; cover.
4. Cook 40 minutes, or until a leaf pulls away easily from base; drain well. Serve with small bowls of melted butter and lemon slices.

CONFETTI VEGETABLE SCRAMBLE
Ready-to-cook frozen vegetables are the starter for this garden-bright medley.

Makes 6 servings.

  1 cup frozen chopped onions (from a 12-ounce bag)
  4 tablespoons (½ stick) butter
  1 cup frozen diced green pepper (from a 10-ounce bag)
  1 package (10 ounces) frozen mixed vegetables
  1 teaspoon salt
  ½ teaspoon Italian seasoning
  3 eggs
  1 package (4 ounces) shredded Cheddar cheese

1. Sauté onions in butter until soft in a large frying pan; stir in pepper and mixed vegetables; cover.
2. Cook 5 minutes; uncover. Stir in salt and Italian seasoning. Cook 5 minutes longer, or until liquid is absorbed.
3. Beat eggs slightly in a small bowl; stir in cheese; pour over vegetables. Cook, stirring constantly, over low heat until eggs set and cheese melts.

SOUFFLÉED BROCCOLI
Sauce topping, tasting like Hollandaise, puffs and turns golden as it heats.

Makes 6 servings.

  1 bunch fresh broccoli (about 2 pounds)
  1 egg white
  ¼ cup mayonnaise or salad dressing
  2 tablespoons Parmesan cheese
  2 teaspoons lemon juice

1. Trim and discard outer leaves and tough ends from broccoli; cut stalks and flowerets into 1-inch pieces. Cook, covered, in small amount of boiling salted water in saucepan just until tender; drain. Arrange in buttered shallow, 6-cup baking dish.
2. Beat egg white until stiff in small bowl; fold in mayonnaise or salad dressing, Parmesan cheese and lemon juice; spoon over broccoli.
3. Slide under broiler 3 minutes to puff topping. Serve immediately.

CASSEROLE PEAS
Here's an easy-to-make, easy-to-serve vegetable idea that's perfect for parties.

Bake at 350° for 25 minutes. Makes 8 servings.

  3 packages (8 ounces each) frozen green peas with cream sauce
  3 tablespoons butter
  2¼ cups milk
  1 cup crunchy nutlike cereal nuggets
  1 cup shredded Cheddar cheese (4 ounces)

1. Prepare peas with butter and milk, following label directions. Mix cereal and cheese in a bowl; set aside ½ cup.
2. Layer one third of the peas into a 7-cup baking dish; sprinkle with half of the remaining cereal mixture. Repeat layers. Spoon remaining peas on top; sprinkle with the ½ cup cereal-cheese mixture.
3. Bake in moderate oven (350°) 25 minutes, or until mixture is bubbly and topping is lightly toasted. Serve immediately.

INDIAN CORN A LA CARTE
Here's a delicious cheese-butter idea you can slather on corn, squash or any other favorite vegetable you enjoy with lots of butter.

Makes 12 servings.

  12 ears of corn with husks
     Parmesan Butter (recipe follows)

1. Peel back husks from corn, leaving stub on; remove all silk. Spread kernels with part of the Parmesan Butter (see below).
2. Pull husks back in place; tie tips with string. Place ears on grill about 6 inches above hot coals.
3. Grill, turning often, 25 minutes, or until kernels are tender. Serve with remaining seasoned butter.
Note: To cook corn in oven, prepare, following Steps 1 and 2. Or remove husks and silk, butter ears and wrap each in a double-thick sheet of foil; place in a large shallow pan. Bake in hot oven (400°), turning often, 25 minutes.

Parmesan Butter: Blend 1 cup (2 sticks) butter, ½ cup grated Parmesan cheese, ½ teaspoon crumbled basil and 1 teaspoon salt in a small bowl. Makes about 1¼ cups.

VEGETABLE CHIVE CHEESE SAUCE
Cheeses are superb for sauce—they melt and blend so beautifully with so many foods.

Makes about 2¼ cups.

  2 tablespoons butter
  2 tablespoons all-purpose flour
  ½ teaspoon salt
  1½ cups milk
  6 ounces chive cream cheese

Melt butter in a medium-size saucepan; stir in flour and salt; cook, stirring constantly, until bubbly. Stir in milk; continue cooking and stirring until sauce thickens and boils 1 minute. Add cheese; stir in until melted. Serve hot over cooked cabbage.

Variation: Caraway Cheese Sauce—Prepare recipe above, substituting 3 long slices caraway cheese for chive cream cheese. Serve hot over cooked green beans. Makes about 2 cups.

8
SALADS

No matter how you toss it, a salad with cheese goes far beyond the ordinary—both in flavor *and* nutrition. Sliced, diced or cubed, cheese is great with greens. Crumbled or shredded, it's a natural with dressings; and spooned into a mound, it's memorable with fruit or gelatin. Of course, there will be days when planning's not your strong point. For these, we recommend sliced tomatoes with, naturally, a blithe sprinkling of cheese on top. It's a last-minute idea, but no matter how you toss it, it's a delicious salad!

BLUE CHEESE FRENCH DRESSING
Try this on any green salad or pour over tomatoes.

Makes 1¼ cups.

⅔ cup vegetable or olive oil
½ cup cider or wine vinegar
½ teaspoon sugar
1 teaspoon salt
¼ teaspoon pepper
⅓ cup coarsely crumbled blue cheese
   (about 1½ ounces)
1 clove garlic, peeled and minced

Combine all ingredients in a screw-top jar with a tight-fitting lid. Shake well to blend; chill.

Variation: Parmesan Dressing—Substitute ½ teaspoon leaf basil, crumbled; ½ teaspoon leaf tarragon, crumbled; and 2 tablespoons grated Parmesan for the blue cheese and garlic in recipe above. Makes 1 cup.

CREAMY BLUE CHEESE DRESSING
This is delicious with almost any tossed green salad or with a fresh shrimp and celery mixture.

Makes about 1½ cups, or enough for 6 servings.

½ cup mayonnaise or salad dressing
½ cup dairy sour cream
½ cup crumbled blue cheese (2 ounces)
1 tablespoon lemon juice
¼ teaspoon salt
   Few drops liquid red-pepper seasoning

Blend all ingredients in a small bowl. Cover; chill. Pour over salad greens.

BLUE CHEESE PEARS
Another switch on fruit and cheese. Stuff pear halves with a nippy filling, put the halves together and coat with walnuts.

Makes 6 servings.

⅓ cup dry cottage cheese or pot cheese
3 or 4 ounces cream cheese
¼ cup mayonnaise or salad dressing
3 tablespoons crumbled blue cheese
1 tablespoon grated lemon rind
   Red food coloring
2 cans (1 pound each) pear halves
1 cup finely chopped walnuts
   Boston lettuce

1. Press cottage cheese through a sieve into a medium-size bowl; beat in cream cheese, mayonnaise or salad dressing, blue cheese and lemon rind. Tint pale pink with food coloring. Chill in the refrigerator at least an hour to season the flavors.

2. Drain syrup from pears into a small bowl; chill to sweeten a fruit beverage.
3. Spoon 1 tablespoon of the cheese mixture into hollow of each of 6 pear halves; top each with a plain pear half. Roll in chopped walnuts on wax paper to coat all over.
4. Line 6 salad plates with lettuce; place a stuffed pear on each; spoon a dollop of remaining cheese mixture on top.

STRAWBERRY PINK DRESSING FOR FRUIT SALADS
Try this on colorful combinations of cottage cheese and fresh fruit, or spoon it over a molded salad.

Makes 1¼ cups.

1 cup whole strawberries
¾ cup cream-style cottage cheese
3 tablespoons lemon juice
2 tablespoons sugar

Combine all ingredients in container of electric blender and whip on high speed until smooth.

CAESAR SALAD
This nationally famous California salad is often used as a first course.

Makes 6 to 8 servings.

2 cloves garlic
¾ cup olive oil
2 cups bread cubes (4 slices)
2 large or 3 small heads romaine lettuce
½ teaspoon freshly ground pepper
½ teaspoon salt
2 medium eggs, soft-cooked for 1 minute
3 tablespoons lemon juice
6 anchovy fillets, drained and cut into small
   pieces (optional)
½ cup freshly grated Parmesan cheese (2 ounces)

1. Cut one of the garlic cloves in half; rub cut surface over inside of a large salad bowl. Discard. Brown remaining garlic clove in ¼ cup of the olive oil in a large skillet. Remove browned garlic clove; add bread cubes; brown on all sides. Drain croutons on paper toweling.
2. Break romaine leaves into bite-size pieces into salad bowl. Sprinkle with pepper and salt. Add remaining olive oil. Mix gently until every piece of lettuce is glistening with oil. Break eggs into the middle of the romaine and pour lemon juice directly over the eggs. Toss gently but thoroughly until there is a creamy look to the salad. Add the anchovies and cheese; taste, adding more salt, pepper and lemon juice, if desired. Go easy on the salt since the Parmesan is salty; toss. Add the croutons and toss again; serve immediately so that the croutons remain crisp.

RAINBOW FRUIT PLATES

Serve this salad for a light lunch or as a backyard dinner buffet special.

Makes 6 servings.

¼ **watermelon, cut lengthwise**
1 **honeydew melon**
  Cottage Cheese Snow (recipe follows)
1 **pint raspberries**
4 **peaches**
  Fresh mint

1. Cut watermelon crosswise into ½-inch-thick slices; pare rind, then cut meat into even-size wedges. (You'll need 3 for each plate.)
2. Halve honeydew melon; scoop out seeds. Cut out enough balls with a melon-ball cutter or ½ teaspoon of a measuring-spoon set to make 3 cups. (Pare any leftover pieces, dice and add to fruit cup for another day.)
3. Make Cottage Cheese Snow. Chill all.
4. When ready to put plates together, wash raspberries and dry. Peel peaches, pit and slice each into 6 crescents.
5. Stand 3 slices of watermelon on each plate; spoon Cottage Cheese Snow into center of plate. Frame with mounds of honeydew balls, raspberries and peach slices. Garnish the cottage cheese mixture with a sprig of fresh mint.

COTTAGE CHEESE SNOW

Fluffy with whipped cream and lightly spiced with ginger, it's a perfect complement to fresh fruits.

Makes 6 servings.

½ **cup heavy cream**
2 **tablespoons sugar**
½ **teaspoon ground ginger**
1 **pound cream-style cottage cheese**
½ **teaspoon grated lemon rind**

Beat cream with sugar and ginger until stiff in a small bowl; fold into cottage cheese and lemon rind in a medium-size bowl. Chill until serving time.

EXTRA-SIMPLE ANTIPASTO SALAD

Save work and table space by making the appetizer and the salad into one colorful dish.

Makes 12 servings.

1 **head romaine, about 1 pound**
1 **can (1 pound, 4 ounces) chick peas**
  Home-style Salad Dressing (recipe follows)
½ **ripe cantaloupe**
¼ **pound thinly sliced salami**
1 **can (4½ ounces) pitted ripe olives, drained**
1 **red pepper, halved, seeded and cubed**
1 **green pepper, halved, seeded and cubed**

1. Wash and trim romaine; drain well. Slice thinly, crosswise. Store in a plastic bag.
2. Drain chick peas and place in a bowl. Add ⅓ cup Home-style Salad Dressing and toss to coat evenly; cover bowl with plastic wrap and chill.
3. When ready to assemble salad: Line a long salad bowl with shredded romaine. Seed and pare cantaloupe; cut into very thin slices and halve.
4. Arrange cantaloupe, salami, chick peas, olives and peppers on lettuce. Pass remaining dressing.

HOME-STYLE SALAD DRESSING

A touch of Parmesan cheese and a dash of Italian herbs give character to this dressing.

Makes about 1 cup.

⅔ **cup vegetable oil**
½ **cup cider vinegar**
2 **tablespoons grated Parmesan cheese**
1 **teaspoon salt**
1 **teaspoon Italian herbs, crumbled**
½ **teaspoon sugar**
¼ **teaspoon pepper**

Combine all ingredients in a jar with a screw top. Shake well. Chill to blend flavors.

MACARONI AND MOZZARELLA SALAD

Pasta needn't be hot to be good, as this savory Italian-style salad proves. It couldn't be easier or more economical to make.

Makes 6 servings.

1 **cup uncooked elbow macaroni**
½ **cup mayonnaise or salad dressing**
¼ **teaspoon leaf oregano, crumbled**
  Pinch leaf thyme
1 **teaspoon dry mustard**
2 **teaspoons salt**
⅛ **teaspoon white pepper**
2 **tablespoons minced onion**
2 **tablespoons minced green pepper**
1 **tablespoon minced, drained pimiento**
¾ **cup finely diced celery**
⅓ **cup finely diced, peeled, seeded cucumber**
1 **cup coarsely shredded mozzarella, Swiss or Cheddar cheese (about 4 ounces)**
3 **hard-cooked eggs, peeled and chopped**

1. Cook macaroni by package directions until firm-tender, adding a drop of vegetable oil to the cooking water to keep macaroni from sticking to itself; drain.
2. Meanwhile, mix together mayonnaise, oregano, thyme, mustard, salt, white pepper, onion, green pepper and pimiento.
3. Place macaroni, celery and cucumber in a large bowl. Add mayonnaise mixture and stir gently to mix. Add cheese and eggs and toss just enough to mix. Chill for about 2 to 3 hours before serving.

EGG AND SWISS CHEESE SALAD
It's tangy egg salad combined with cheese.

Makes 4 servings.

6 hard-cooked eggs, coarsely chopped
6 ounces Swiss cheese slices, cut in slivers
⅓ cup mayonnaise or salad dressing
1 tablespoon mustard with horseradish
¼ cup chopped green pepper
2 tablespoons chopped pimiento
½ teaspoon salt
⅛ teaspoon pepper
Salad greens

1. Combine eggs, cheese, mayonnaise or salad dressing, mustard, green pepper, pimiento, salt and pepper in a large bowl. Toss lightly to coat. Chill.
2. Serve on crisp salad greens with a sprinkling of chopped chives, if you wish.

BAVARIAN BAKED POTATO SALAD
This warm robust salad is chock-full of chunky frankfurters and cheese.

Makes 6 servings.

5 medium-size potatoes (about 2 pounds)
1 pound frankfurters, cut into 1-inch pieces
2 tablespoons vegetable oil
1 medium-size onion, chopped (½ cup)
2 tablespoons all-purpose flour
3 tablespoons brown sugar
1 teaspoon salt
1 teaspoon dry mustard
⅛ teaspoon pepper
1 cup water
⅓ cup vinegar
1 cup thinly sliced celery
½ cup chopped green pepper
¼ cup chopped pimiento
8 ounces Cheddar cheese, sliced

1. Cook potatoes in boiling salted water in a large saucepan 30 minutes, or until tender; drain. Cool until easy to handle, then peel and dice. Place in a medium-size bowl.
2. Brown frankfurters in oil in a skillet; remove with a slotted spoon to the bowl with potatoes.
3. Sauté onion in same skillet until soft. Combine flour, sugar, salt and dry mustard; stir into drippings; cook, stirring constantly, until bubbly. Stir in water and vinegar; continue cooking and stirring until dressing thickens and bubbles 1 minute.
4. Add celery, green pepper and pimiento; cook 1 minute longer. Pour over potatoes and frankfurters. Spoon one half of the potato mixture into an 8-cup baking dish; layer with 4 slices of cheese; spoon remaining potato mixture into dish. Top with remaining cheese slices cut into triangles.
5. Bake in moderate oven (350°) 15 minutes, or until cheese is slightly melted. Serve salad warm.

CHEF'S SALAD
This hearty meat-and-vegetable salad is always a favorite. Try it with warm buttered bread.

Makes 6 servings.

1 chicken breast, weighing about 12 ounces
2 cups water
Few celery tops
1 small onion, halved
1½ teaspoons salt
¾ cup chili sauce
½ cup mayonnaise or salad dressing
1 teaspoon instant minced onion
½ teaspoon sugar
1 package (3½ ounces) sliced tongue, rolled in cone shapes
1 package (8 ounces) sliced cooked ham, cut in thin strips
8 ounces sliced Swiss cheese, cut in thin strips
1 large tomato, cut into wedges
1 small cucumber, pared and thinly sliced
1 hard-cooked egg, sieved
6 cups broken mixed salad greens

1. Combine chicken breast, water, celery, onion and 1 teaspoon of the salt in a medium-size saucepan; heat to boiling; cover. Simmer 30 minutes, or until chicken is tender. Remove from broth; cool. Chill about 45 minutes. Skin and bone, then cut chicken into bite-size cubes.
2. Blend chili sauce, mayonnaise or salad dressing, instant minced onion, sugar and remaining ½ teaspoon salt in a small bowl. Chill dressing for about 30 minutes.
3. Place greens in a large salad bowl. Arrange tongue, ham, chicken, Swiss cheese, tomatoes and cucumber slices in sections on top. Sprinkle the sieved egg over all.
4. Just before serving, spoon on dressing; toss.

SUNDAY-SUPPER SALAD
This cheese and vegetable salad has a surprise flavor ingredient . . . pretzels.

Makes 8 servings.

1 small head iceberg lettuce, broken in bite-size pieces
1 small head romaine, broken in bite-size pieces
1 large cucumber, pared and sliced
1 large green pepper, halved, seeded and sliced
10 ounces sharp Cheddar cheese, cut in ¼-inch cubes
1 package (8 ounces) sliced caraway cheese, cut in thin strips
1 teaspoon coriander seeds
1 teaspoon cumin seeds
6 peppercorns
1 egg
½ cup bottled Italian salad dressing
1 cup broken pretzels

1. Place lettuce and romaine in a large salad bowl; top with cucumber and green pepper. Pile Cheddar-cheese cubes in a mound in center; place caraway-cheese strips in a ring around Cheddar.
2. Crush coriander and cumin seeds and peppercorns; sprinkle over salad mixture. (To speed the job, fold seeds and peppercorns in a double-thick sheet of wax paper; crush with a rolling pin.)
3. Place egg in boiling water in a small saucepan; cover; remove from heat. Let stand only 2 minutes.
4. Break egg into a cup, then place in center of salad mixture; drizzle dressing over all; add pretzels. Toss to mix well.

PERUVIAN POTATO SALAD
This salad is one chili-pepper fans will love.

Makes 8 servings.

 6 medium-size potatoes, pared and cubed (6 cups)
 2 hard-cooked eggs, shelled
 1 cup shredded Cheddar cheese (4 ounces)
 1 small onion, chopped fine (¼ cup)
 1 jalapeño or green chili pepper, chopped fine
 1 teaspoon salt
 2 tablespoons olive or vegetable oil
 ½ cup light cream
    Iceberg lettuce

1. Cook potatoes in boiling salted water in a large saucepan 15 minutes, or until tender; drain. Return potatoes to pan and shake over low heat until dry and fluffy. Place in a large bowl.
2. While potatoes cook, mash eggs in a small bowl; stir in cheese, onion, pepper and salt. Slowly stir in olive oil until well-blended, then cream. Pour over warm potatoes, toss until evenly coated.
3. Chill about an hour to season. Serve in a large lettuce-lined salad bowl.

SHRIMPS HAWAIIAN
Sweet shrimps contrast pleasingly with tangy pineapple in a creamy dressing.

Makes 6 servings.

 2 cans (about 5 ounces each) deveined shrimps
 1 can (about 14 ounces) pineapple chunks
 1 can (5 ounces) water chestnuts
 6 cups broken salad greens
 ½ cup mayonnaise or salad dressing
 ¼ cup crumbled blue cheese (about 1 ounce)

1. Drain shrimps. Drain syrup from pineapple chunks into a cup and reserve syrup for Step 3. Drain water chestnuts, then chop coarsely.
2. Place salad greens in a large bowl; pile shrimps, pineapple and water chestnuts in rows on top.
3. Blend 2 tablespoons of the saved pineapple syrup into mayonnaise or salad dressing and blue cheese in a small bowl; drizzle over salad; toss.

SALATA
"Salata" is the Greek word for salad—and this one comes complete with the feta cheese—made here from cow's milk instead of the goat's milk used traditionally in Greece.

Makes 6 servings.

 1 small head Boston lettuce
 ¼ cup chopped green onions or scallions
 2 medium-size potatoes, cooked, peeled and sliced (2 cups)
 2 cups cherry tomatoes, sliced
 2 cans (2 ounces each) flat anchovy fillets
 ¼ cup coarsely chopped parsley
 1 bunch radishes, trimmed and sliced
 ½ cup crumbled feta cheese
 1 cup Greek olives or 1 cup pitted ripe olives, halved
 ¼ cup olive or vegetable oil
 2 tablespoons lemon juice
 ½ teaspoon leaf oregano, crumbled
 ½ teaspoon salt
    Freshly ground pepper

1. Line a large deep platter or shallow bowl with lettuce leaves, then break remainder into bite-size pieces and place in center; sprinkle green onions over lettuce.
2. Layer potatoes, tomatoes, anchovies, parsley, radishes and cheese on top. Place olives in a ring around base; garnish cheese with a wedge of lemon, if you wish.
3. Combine olive oil, lemon juice, oregano, salt and pepper in a jar with a tight lid; shake well to mix.
4. Just before serving, drizzle dressing over vegetable mixture; toss lightly to mix.

TUNA SUPPER SALAD
It's hearty with tuna, cheese and limas seasoned with spicy French dressing.

Makes 6 servings.

 2 cans (about 7 ounces each) tuna, drained and broken up
 2 tablespoons lemon juice
 ¼ teaspoon seasoned pepper
 1 can (1 pound) lima beans, drained
 ¼ cup bottled French dressing
 6 cups broken salad greens
 4 slices Muenster cheese, cut in strips
 12 pitted ripe olives, quartered

1. Toss tuna lightly with lemon juice and seasoned pepper in a small bowl. Toss limas with French dressing in a second small bowl. Chill both to season and blend flavors.
2. Place salad greens in a large bowl; pile tuna, limas, cheese strips and olives in rows, spoke fashion, on top. Garnish with pimiento strips and cashew nuts, if you wish. Toss, salad style, at the table, adding more French dressing, if you wish.

FAMILY CHEF'S SALAD

Mild and sharp cheeses, one-bite tomatoes and hard-cooked eggs make this big-bowl winner.

Makes 6 servings.

    1 large head romaine, broken into bite-size pieces
    1 small head iceberg lettuce, broken into bite-size pieces
    ½ head chicory, broken into bite-size pieces
    ⅓ cup grated Parmesan cheese
    8 ounces sliced Swiss cheese, cut in strips
    8 ounces sliced Cheddar cheese, cut in strips
    3 hard-cooked eggs, shelled and cut in wedges
    1 cup cherry tomatoes, halved
      Watercress
    ½ cup bottled oil-and-vinegar salad dressing

1. Combine romaine, lettuce and chicory in a large salad bowl. Set aside 1 tablespoon of the Parmesan cheese for dressing in Step 3; sprinkle remaining over the greens.
2. Arrange Swiss and Cheddar cheese strips, spoke fashion, in 6 piles on top of greens; place egg wedges and tomatoes between spokes; place a cluster of watercress in center.
3. Just before serving, mix salad dressing with remaining Parmesan cheese in a cup; drizzle over salad; toss to mix.

CARROUSEL MACARONI BOWL

Presto! Favorite macaroni-and-cheese turns into a cool salad. Cubes of ham and crisp peas add an unusually flavorful touch.

Makes 6 servings.

    1 package (8 ounces) elbow macaroni
    2 tablespoons salad oil
    2 tablespoons cider vinegar
    1 tablespoon grated onion
    ½ teaspoon seasoned salt
    ½ teaspoon dry mustard
    ¼ teaspoon seasoned pepper
    1 cup grated Cheddar cheese (4 ounces)
    ½ cup mayonnaise or salad dressing
    1 cup diced cooked ham
    1 pound fresh peas, shelled (1 cup)
    ½ cup chopped celery
    4 cups broken salad greens
      Green-pepper strips
      Pimiento strips

1. Cook macaroni in a large saucepan, following label directions; drain well. Return to same pan.
2. While still hot, drizzle salad oil and vinegar over; sprinkle with onion, seasoned salt, mustard and seasoned pepper; toss to mix well. Add cheese and toss again until cheese melts.
3. Spoon into a large bowl; cover; chill. (Or let the macaroni mixture stand at room temperature for awhile if you prefer salad not too chilled.)

4. When ready to serve, fold in mayonnaise or salad dressing, ham, uncooked peas and celery.
5. Partly fill a large casserole or bowl with salad greens; spoon macaroni-salad mixture on top. Garnish with green pepper and pimiento.

HAM-AND-EGG CROWN

All kinds of good nutrition—and flavor—are molded into this salad.

Makes 8 servings.

    3 envelopes unflavored gelatin
    3 envelopes instant chicken broth
    2 tablespoons sugar
    2 teaspoons salt
    4¼ cups cold water
    ¼ cup lemon juice
    ¼ teaspoon liquid red-pepper seasoning
    1 cup mayonnaise or salad dressing
    1 tablespoon prepared mustard
    6 hard-cooked eggs, shelled
    1 can or jar (4 ounces) pimientos, drained and diced
    ½ cup diced celery
    ½ cup diced green pepper
    1 package (about 4 ounces) sliced boiled ham
    1 container (4 ounces) whipped cream cheese with chives
      Watercress

1. Mix gelatin, chicken broth, sugar and salt in a small saucepan; stir in 2 cups of the water. Heat slowly, stirring constantly, until gelatin dissolves; remove from heat. Stir in 2 more cups water, lemon juice and red-pepper seasoning.
2. Measure 1 cup of the gelatin mixture into a small bowl; stir in remaining ¼ cup water; pour into an 8-cup mold. Chill about 20 minutes, or until as thick as unbeaten egg white.
3. Beat mayonnaise or salad dressing and mustard into remaining gelatin mixture; pour into a shallow pan. Freeze about 20 minutes, or until firm 1 inch in from edges, but still soft in center.
4. Slice eggs. Pick out 8 of the prettiest center slices; dice remainder. Arrange slices in a ring in thickened gelatin layer in mold; let stand just until gelatin is sticky-firm.
5. Spoon mayonnaise-gelatin mixture into a large bowl; beat until fluffy-smooth. Fold in pimientos, celery, green pepper and diced eggs. Carefully spoon over sticky-firm layer in mold. Chill at least 4 hours, or overnight, until firm.
6. Several hours before serving, spread each ham slice with cream cheese. Starting at short end, roll up, jelly-roll fashion; wrap in wax paper; chill.
7. When ready to serve, run a sharp-tip thin-blade knife around top of salad to loosen; dip mold very quickly in and out of hot water. Cover mold with a large serving plate; turn upside down; lift off mold.
8. Cut each ham roll into 6 slices; stand around salad; garnish with sprigs of fresh watercress.

COTTAGE APPLE SALAD
The tart creamy dressing adds new flavor to a favorite fruit salad.

Makes 6 servings.

- **4 medium-size apples, quartered, cored and diced**
- **½ cup golden raisins**
- **½ cup chopped walnuts**
- **1 tablespoon sugar**
- **1 tablespoon lemon juice**
- **¼ cup cream-style cottage cheese**
- **¼ cup dairy sour cream**

1. Combine apples, raisins and walnuts in medium-size bowl; sprinkle sugar and lemon juice over; toss.
2. Blend cottage cheese and sour cream in 1-cup measure; spoon over apple mixture; toss lightly.

TWO-CHEESE SALAD
Two kinds of cheese combine with two varieties of greens to make a double-good salad.

Makes 6 servings.

- **1 small head romaine**
- **1 small head iceberg lettuce**
- **¼ pound sharp Cheddar cheese, cubed**
- **¼ pound Monterey Jack cheese, cubed or ¼ pound Muenster cheese, cubed**
- **6 small thin carrots, trimmed and scraped**
- **6 white radishes, trimmed and scraped**
- **Piquant Dressing (recipe follows)**

1. Break romaine and lettuce into bite-size pieces in individual salad bowls, leaving a shallow well in center of each. Arrange cheese cubes around well.
2. Bunch carrots and radishes, tip ends up, to form a bouquet; place in center well. (Cheese cubes will hold bouquet in place.)
3. Serve Piquant Dressing and have each person add his own dressing.

Piquant Dressing: Combine ⅔ cup salad oil, ⅓ cup wine vinegar or cider vinegar, 2 teaspoons sugar, ½ teaspoon dry mustard and ½ teaspoon salt in jar with tight-fitting cover. Shake well to mix; chill; then shake again just before serving. Makes 1 cup.

PINEAPPLE-CUCUMBER SALAD
Tangy fruit, cucumber and cream cheese blend into a refreshing topper for lettuce wedges.

Makes 6 servings.

- **3 or 4 ounces cream cheese**
- **1 can (about 8 ounces) crushed pineapple, drained**
- **½ cup finely chopped pared cucumber**
- **¼ teaspoon salt**
- **1 medium-size head iceberg lettuce**

1. Soften cream cheese in a medium-size bowl; stir in drained pineapple, cucumber and salt. (If made ahead, chill until serving time, then remove from refrigerator about ½ hour before serving.)
2. Cut lettuce into 6 wedges; place on salad plates. Spoon cheese mixture over.

CONFETTI CAULIFLOWER BOWL
Here's an unusual approach to making salad—the crisp vegetables are part of the dressing.

Makes 6 servings.

- **1 large head iceberg lettuce**
- **½ head small cauliflower**
- **½ cup bottled Italian salad dressing**
- **2 tablespoons minced radishes**
- **2 tablespoons minced carrot**
- **2 tablespoons minced green onion**
- **½ cup shredded Cheddar cheese (about 2 ounces)**

1. Trim lettuce; wash; drain. Wrap in towel to absorb moisture. Chill several hours.
2. Trim and remove core from cauliflower; separate into flowerets. Wash; drain; dry. Cut each floweret lengthwise into very thin slices (about 1½ cups).
3. Mix salad dressing, radishes, carrot and green onion in a pie plate; add cauliflower; turn to coat well. Chill, turning several times, at least 1 hour.
4. When ready to serve, break lettuce into bite-size pieces in a large salad bowl. (You should have about 6 cups.) Sprinkle cheese over top. Spoon dressing with vegetables over all. Toss lightly to coat.

FRUIT SAMPLER
It's a sunny roundup of fruits topped with a mellow cheese-rich dressing.

Makes 4 servings.

- **1 small head of leaf lettuce**
- **2 oranges, peeled and sliced crosswise**
- **2 pears, pared and sliced**
- **2 nectarines, sliced**
- **2 sweet yellow plums, halved and pitted**
- **½ cup boysenberries or raspberries**
- **2 tablespoons sugar**
- **⅛ teaspoon ground ginger**
- **Camembert Cream (recipe follows)**

1. Line 4 salad plates with lettuce.
2. Arrange orange, pear and nectarine slices in separate mounds around edge of each plate, dividing evenly. Place a plum half in middle, hollow side up; mound berries on top.
3. Mix sugar and ginger in a small cup; sprinkle over fruits; chill. Serve with Camembert Cream.

Camembert Cream: Mash 2⅔ ounces Camembert cheese with fork in small bowl; slowly blend in ¼ cup heavy cream. Makes ¾ cup.

ORANGE-PEAR ROSETTE
Cheese filling doubles as dressing in this two-fruit salad-dessert.

Makes 4 servings at 94 calories each.

1⅓ ounces Camembert cheese
2 tablespoons cream-style cottage cheese
2 medium-size fresh ripe pears
1 can (about 11 ounces) diet-pack
   mandarin-orange segments, drained
   Grated orange rind

1. Mash Camembert cheese in a small bowl; blend in cottage cheese; chill.
2. Just before serving, halve pears lengthwise and core.
3. Place a half on each of four serving plates; spoon cheese mixture into hollows. Arrange six mandarin-orange segments, petal fashion, around cheese in each; sprinkle with grated orange rind. (Save any remaining mandarin-orange segments for another day.) Weight-watcher's serving: One pear half, 6 mandarin-orange segments and 1 rounded teaspoonful cheese mixture.

MAIN-DISH POTATO SALAD A LA PELOPONNESE
This marvelous money-stretching Greek recipe has cheese enough to boost it into the main-dish category. Greeks make it with feta, a crumbly, creamy-white, refreshingly salty goat cheese; use the feta cheese or, if you like, substitute with cottage cheese.

Makes 6 servings.

2 pounds new potatoes, boiled until fork-tender,
   peeled and sliced fairly thin
2 tablespoons minced parsley
1 stalk celery, minced
1 small onion, peeled and minced
½ cup diced black or green (preferably Greek)
   olives
1 tablespoon grated Parmesan cheese
¼ teaspoon dillweed
   Pinch leaf rosemary, crumbled
1 teaspoon salt
¼ teaspoon freshly ground black pepper
   Juice of 1 lemon
2 tablespoons olive oil
¼ cup mayonnaise or salad dressing
8 ounces cream-style cottage cheese
⅓ to ½ cup milk (enough for good consistency)
6 tomato cups (optional)

1. Mix together potatoes, 1 tablespoon of the minced parsley and all remaining ingredients except tomato cups; cover and let "mellow" in refrigerator 2 hours or more.
2. Toss salad again, well; mound onto plates or, if you like, in tomato cups and sprinkle with the remaining tablespoon minced parsley.

Right: Shrimp Louis Salad combines a classic Louis dressing with shrimp, avocado, cucumber and greens. Recipe is on this page.

AVOCADO-PAPAYA FRUIT PLATES
Ham and cheese strips plus a stuffed egg top a base of avocado, tomato and papaya slices.

Makes 6 servings.

1 head iceberg lettuce, shredded fine
3 medium-size avocados, halved lengthwise,
   peeled, seeded and sliced
3 medium-size tomatoes, cut in wedges
2 medium-size papayas, cut in 6 one-inch-thick
   rings, then pared and seeded
½ pound sliced cooked ham, cut in thin strips
8 ounces sliced Cheddar cheese,
   cut in thin strips
   Stuffed Salad Eggs (recipe follows)
   Pineapple Dressing (recipe follows)

1. Mound lettuce, dividing evenly, onto 6 individual serving plates; alternate avocado and tomato slices in a ring around edge.
2. Top with a papaya slice, then strips of ham and cheese. Garnish with a Stuffed Salad Egg. Serve with Pineapple Dressing.

Stuffed Salad Eggs: Hard-cook 3 eggs; shell, then halve lengthwise. Scoop out yolks and mash in a small bowl. Blend in 1 tablespoon mayonnaise or salad dressing, ½ teaspoon prepared mustard and salt and pepper to taste. Pile back into whites. Garnish with parsley. Chill. Makes 6 servings.

Pineapple Dressing: Blend ½ cup bottled cole-slaw dressing, ¼ cup drained crushed pineapple (from an 8-ounce can) and 2 tablespoons lemon juice in a small bowl; chill. Makes about ¾ cup.

SHRIMP LOUIS SALAD
Creamy make-ahead dressing and a few basic salad ingredients bring about some spectacular results.

Makes about 1⅓ cups dressing, or enough for 8 servings of salad.

1 cup cream-style cottage cheese
1 hard-cooked egg, peeled and halved
¼ cup tomato juice
1 teaspoon prepared mustard
1 pound shrimp, cooked, peeled and deveined
1 avocado, peeled and sliced
1 cucumber, sliced
2 ripe olives, halved
   Assorted salad greens (we used about ½
   head chicory and romaine)

1. Combine cottage cheese, egg, tomato juice and mustard in container of electric blender; whirl until smooth. Cover; chill until serving time.
2. Combine shrimp, avocado, cucumber, olives and greens in large salad bowl; toss gently. Pour chilled dressing over and toss again until well mixed. Garnish with lemon wedges, if you wish.

JELLIED FRUIT RING

With its spicy-sweet cream dressing, it's a partylike salad.

Makes 6 servings.

1 package (6 ounces) strawberry-flavor gelatin
2 cups hot water
2 bottles (7 ounces each) ginger ale
2 tablespoons lemon juice
2 medium-size firm ripe bananas
1 can (about 9 ounces) sliced peaches, drained
1 can (8 ounces) pear halves, drained
  and halved lengthwise
  Honey Cream Dressing (recipe follows)

1. Dissolve gelatin in hot water in a medium-size bowl; stir in ginger ale and lemon juice. Chill just until as thick as unbeaten egg white, then keep at room temperature while layering mold.
2. Place a 5-cup ring mold in a pan partly filled with ice and water; pour ½ cup of the gelatin mixture into mold.
3. Peel 1 banana and cut diagonally into thin slices; set other banana aside for Step 7. Arrange slices in a ring in gelatin mixture in mold; let set a few minutes, or until sticky-firm, then carefully spoon ¾ cup more gelatin mixture over bananas. Let set again until sticky-firm.
4. Pour 2 more cups of the gelatin mixture into mold; press part of the drained peach slices and pear quarters down into gelatin around edge of mold to make a pretty pattern; let the gelatin set until it's sticky-firm.
5. Cut any remaining peaches and pears into cubes; fold into remaining gelatin mixture in bowl; spoon into mold. Remove from pan of ice; chill several hours, or overnight, or until firm.
6. To umold, run a sharp-tip thin-blade knife around top of mold, then dip mold very quickly in and out of a pan of hot water. Cover mold with serving plate; turn upside down, then gently lift off mold.
7. Peel and slice remaining banana; arrange in a ring on top of salad. Serve with Honey Cream Dressing (recipe follows).

HONEY CREAM DRESSING

Cottage cheese blends with allspice, honey and nuts for this fruit-salad topper.

Makes 1¼ cups.

1 cup (8 ounces) cream-style cottage cheese
¼ cup chopped pecans
4 tablespoons light cream
1 tablespoon honey
¼ teaspoon ground allspice

Press cottage cheese through a sieve into a small bowl; stir in remaining ingredients. Cover; chill. Stir well again just before serving.

SUN-GLOW CORONET

Its triple layers blend a sparkling vegetable top and bottom with creamy cheese between.

Makes 6 servings.

2 packages (3 ounces each) orange-flavor gelatin
2 cups hot water
1½ cups cold water
2 tablespoons lemon juice
2 large carrots, pared
3 ounces Neufchâtel cheese
½ cup diced celery
2 tablespoons sliced stuffed green olives

1. Dissolve both packages of gelatin in hot water in a medium-size bowl; stir in cold water and lemon juice. Measure 1½ cups into a 6-cup mold.
2. Place mold in a pan of ice and water to speed setting; chill until as thick as unbeaten egg white. Keep bowl of remaining gelatin mixture at room temperature while layering mold.
3. While layer chills, slice one of the carrots ⅛-inch thick; cut slices into tiny flower shapes with a truffle or aspic cutter; or, shape flowers with a knife. Grate enough of remaining carrot to make ½ cup.
4. Arrange carrot flowers in thickened gelatin in mold to make a pattern; chill until sticky-firm.
5. Beat 1 cup of the remaining gelatin mixture into cheese until well blended in a small bowl; spoon over layer in mold; chill until sticky-firm.
6. Chill remaining gelatin in bowl until as thick as unbeaten egg white; fold in grated carrot, celery and olives; carefully spoon over sticky-firm cheese layer. Remove from ice and water; chill in refrigerator several hours, or until firm. (Overnight is best.)
7. When ready to serve, run a sharp-tip thin-blade knife around top of salad to loosen; dip mold very quickly in and out of hot water. Cover mold with a large serving plate; turn upside down; gently lift off mold. Frame with crisp salad greens and serve with mayonnaise or salad dressing, if you wish.

WINTER SALAD

This is especially good with a homemade soup.

Makes 6 servings.

2 packages frozen succotash
3 tablespoons salad or olive oil
3 tablespoons wine vinegar
1½ teaspoons seasoned salt
  Salad greens
¾ cup sliced celery
1 cup cubed Cheddar cheese (4 ounces)

1. Cook succotash, following label directions; drain. Place in medium-size bowl; toss lightly with oil, vinegar and seasoned salt. Chill.
2. Fill salad bowl with bite-size pieces of salad greens; top with celery, cheese and marinated vegetables; toss just before serving.

9
DESSERTS

Cheese and fruit may seem like a simple offering to the uninitiated. But to anyone who loves a light, flavorful dessert, the combination is hard to beat. Unless, of course, you've just made a cheesecake adorned with fruit and a beautiful sweet glaze. Or perhaps you'd prefer an apple pie with your cheese. The possibilities go on and on, never failing to please when one of the ingredients is cheese. Turn the page and begin to discover your own favorite, very special desserts.

THE DESSERT TRAY

A dessert cheese tray can include an unlimited number of cheeses. However, for most occasions four varieties are ample. These, as suggested by the menus below, should range from mild to sharp and from soft to semi-hard. Serve them with fresh fruit (apples, pears and grapes are the three most popular choices), plus some Italian or French bread and crackers.

Incidentally, don't forget to remove the cheese from the refrigerator ahead of time. An hour at room temperature is recommended for most, although the soft cheeses such as Camembert and Brie can be mellowed for as many as eight hours before serving.

Dessert Tray 1
The cheese: Neufchâtel, Bel Paese, provolone and gorgonzola.
The fruit: Pears, apples, grapes and melon.
Dessert Tray 2
The cheese: Camembert, Cheddar, Edam and Stilton.
The fruit: Apples, grapes, peaches and plums.
Dessert Tray 3
The cheese: Brick, Swiss, provolone and Liederkranz.
The fruit: Apricots, apples, pears and melon.
Dessert Tray 4
The cheese: Blue, Brie, Cheddar.
The fruit: Pears, apples, cherries and plums.
Dessert Tray 5
The cheese: Gouda, cream, brick and provolone.
The fruit: Nectarines, apples, pineapple and oranges.

Page 133:
Three spectacular cheese desserts include, from top to bottom: Pineapple Cheesecake, Frozen Blueberry Ripple Cheesecake and Viennese Fruit Tart. Serve them with Plantation Eggnog. The recipes for all are in this chapter.

PLANTATION EGGNOG
This creamy drink has plenty of "punch." For a really delectable dessert, serve it with cheesecake, as pictured on page 133.

Makes 20 punch-cup servings.

    9 eggs
    1 cup super-fine sugar
    2 cups bourbon
    ½ cup Cognac
    2 cups milk
    3 cups heavy cream
       Ground nutmeg

1. Separate eggs, placing yolks in a large bowl and whites in a second large bowl.
2. Add sugar to egg yolks; beat until fluffy-thick. Stir in bourbon, Cognac and milk. Chill in refrigerator several hours, or until very cold.
3. Beat egg whites until they stand in firm peaks. Beat heavy cream until stiff in a large bowl. Fold beaten egg whites, then whipped cream, into egg-yolk mixture; pour into large punch bowl. Sprinkle with nutmeg. Ladle into individual punch cups.

VIENNESE FRUIT TART
Jelly-glazed fruits and a creamy no-cook filling put this dessert in the quick-but-elegant class.

Makes 8 servings.

    1 can (6 ounces) frozen orange juice concentrate
    1 nine-and-a-half-inch packaged sponge cake layer (6 ounces) or 1 nine-inch baked pastry shell
    3 ounces cream cheese, softened to room temperature
    2 cans (5 ounces each) vanilla pudding
    1 can (1 pound) apricot halves, well-drained
    1 pint fresh strawberries, halved
    ½ pound (1 cup) seedless green grapes
    1 can (12½ ounces) mandarin orange slices, well-drained
    ½ cup apple jelly

1. Heat orange juice concentrate in a small saucepan just until hot.
2. Place cake on serving dish; brush generously with orange juice.
3. Stir cream cheese until very soft in a small bowl; stir in pudding. Spread mixture onto the bottom of cake layer.
4. Arrange halved and sliced fruit in a decorative pattern on top of pudding mixture. (See photograph on page 133 as a guide.) Heat apple jelly in a small saucepan until melted; brush over all fruits. Chill.

FROZEN BLUEBERRY RIPPLE CHEESECAKE
Easy to make, cool and frosty, this big cheesecake has a generous swirl of sweet blueberries running through.

Makes 12 servings.

    ¾ cup graham cracker crumbs
    2 tablespoons sugar
    3 tablespoons butter, melted
    1 cup sugar
    ⅓ cup water
    ⅛ teaspoon cream of tartar
    3 egg whites
    1 pound (16 ounces) cream cheese
    ½ cup dairy sour cream
    2 teaspoons vanilla
    1 tablespoon grated lemon rind
    ½ cup blueberry preserves
       Whipped cream
       Fresh or frozen unsweetened blueberries

1. Combine crumbs, sugar and butter in a small bowl; blend well. Press firmly over bottom of an 8-inch spring-form pan. Chill.
2. Combine sugar, water and cream of tartar in a small saucepan; bring to boiling. Boil rapidly 8 to 10 minutes, or until syrup registers 236° on a candy thermometer (or until syrup spins a 2-inch thread when dropped from spoon).

3. Meanwhile in large bowl of electric mixer, beat egg whites until stiff peaks form; pour hot syrup in a thin stream over egg whites while beating constantly. Continue beating until very stiff peaks form and mixture cools, altogether about 15 minutes.

4. Beat cream cheese and sour cream until light and fluffy; beat in vanilla and lemon rind. Add ¼ of meringue to cheese mixture; stir to combine well. Fold remaining meringue into cheese mixture until no streaks of meringue and cheese remain.

5. Spoon about ¼ of cheese mixture into prepared pan; drizzle part of blueberry preserves over. Continue to layer cheese mixture and preserves this way. Freeze overnight, or until firm.

6. Decorate with whipped cream and blueberries.

PINEAPPLE CHEESECAKE
A deluxe pineapple version of the velvety-rich Lindy's cheesecake.

Bake at 475° for 12 minutes, then at 250° for 1½ hours. Makes 16 servings.

½ recipe Cooky Crust (recipe follows)
2½ pounds cream cheese
1¾ cups sugar
3 tablespoons all-purpose flour
1 teaspoon vanilla
5 eggs
2 egg yolks
¼ cup heavy cream
 Pineapple Glaze (recipe follows)
 Maraschino cherries

1. Roll ⅓ of chilled Cooky Crust dough to cover the bottom of a 10-inch spring-form pan.
2. Bake in hot oven (400°) for 8 minutes, or until crust is lightly browned; cool. Grease sides of the spring-form pan; roll remaining dough into 2 strips about 15 inches long and 2½ inches wide; press onto sides of pan and fit together with bottom. Refrigerate until filling is prepared.
3. Let cream cheese soften in a large bowl; blend in sugar, flour and vanilla. Beat with electric mixer until light and fluffy. Add eggs and egg yolks, one at a time, beating well after each addition; stir in heavy cream; pour into crust.
4. Bake in very hot oven (475°) 12 minutes; lower temperature to 250° and bake 1½ hours longer. Turn off oven; let cake remain in oven 1 hour.
5. Remove from oven; cool on a wire rack; loosen around edge with a knife; release spring and remove side of pan. Spread Pineapple Glaze on top of cake; decorate with maraschino cherries as shown in the photograph on pages 132–133.

Pineapple Glaze—Combine 3 tablespoons sugar and 1 tablespoon cornstarch in a small saucepan. Slowly stir in contents of a 1 pound, 4 ounce can of crushed pineapple. Cook, stirring constantly, over medium heat, until mixture thickens and bubbles 1 minute; cool and spread on Pineapple Cheesecake.

COOKY CRUST

2 cups sifted all-purpose flour
½ cup sugar
¾ cup (1½ sticks) butter, softened
2 egg yolks, slightly beaten
1 teaspoon vanilla

Mix flour and sugar together in a medium-size bowl; cut in butter with a pastry blender until mixture is crumbly. Add egg yolks and vanilla; mix lightly with a fork just until pastry holds together and leaves side of bowl clean. Chill until ready to use.
Note: For half the recipe, use 1 cup flour, ¼ cup sugar, 6 tablespoons butter, 1 egg yolk and ½ teaspoon vanilla extract.

MANDARIN CREAM CAKE
Your refrigerator "bakes" this rich chiffonlike treat.

Bake shell at 375° for 10 minutes. Makes 12 servings.

1½ cups crushed whole-wheat cereal flakes
4 tablespoons sugar
4 tablespoons (½ stick) butter, softened
1 package (3 ounces) lemon-flavor gelatin
8 ounces cream cheese
1 jar (about 11 ounces) mandarin-orange segments
1 cup heavy cream
2 tablespoons sugar

1. Blend cereal flakes with sugar and butter in a small bowl; set aside ⅓ cup for topping. Press remaining over bottom and up sides of a 4-cup shallow baking dish. Bake in moderate oven (375°) 10 minutes, or until set; cool completely on a wire rack.
2. Dissolve gelatin in 1 cup hot water in a large bowl; stir in cream cheese until smooth; chill until as thick as unbeaten egg whites.
3. While mixture chills, drain mandarin-orange segments; set aside 36 segments for topping; fold remaining into thickened gelatin mixture.
4. Beat cream with 2 tablespoons sugar until stiff in a bowl; fold into gelatin mixture; spoon into shell.
5. Arrange 12 circles on top of gelatin mixture, using 3 mandarin-orange segments for each; spoon remaining cereal mixture in centers. Chill until firm.

FLUFFY LEMON CREAM
This topping is delightful on warm gingerbread.

Makes 1⅓ cups.

8 ounces cream cheese, softened
½ cup sifted 10X (confectioners' powdered) sugar
¼ cup light cream
½ teaspoon lemon extract

Blend cream cheese, sugar, cream and lemon extract together in a small bowl. Chill slightly and serve as topping on gingerbread or spice cake.

135

FRUIT AND CHEESE FONDUE
Here's a beautiful change-of-pace from the classic fruit and cheese dessert. (Shown at left.)

Makes 6 to 8 servings.

      2 tablespoons butter
      2 tablespoons all-purpose flour
    ½ teaspoon salt
    ½ teaspoon nutmeg
  1½ cups milk
      2 cups shredded Cheddar cheese (8 ounces)
    ⅓ cup crumbled blue cheese (about 2 ounces)

1. Melt butter in a large saucepan; stir in flour, salt and nutmeg to form a smooth paste. Remove from heat; gradually stir in milk. Return to heat and cook over medium heat, stirring constantly, until smooth and thickened; continue cooking and stirring 2 minutes longer.
2. Remove from heat; stir in Cheddar and blue cheese. If necessary, return to heat to finish melting cheese, but do not boil.
3. Pour melted cheese mixture into fondue pot; keep warm. Serve with sliced apples and pears, orange sections, honeydew or cantaloupe chunks and balls, pineapple wedges or grapes. Let guests spear fruits with long-handled fondue forks and dip into the hot cheese mixture.

APRICOT MELBA TARTS
A cheese-rich filling teams up with canned fruit.

Bake at 425° for 12 minutes. Makes 8 tarts.

      1 package piecrust mix
      1 package (about 3 ounces) vanilla pudding
        and pie filling mix
  1½ cups milk
      8 ounces cream cheese, cut up
      1 can (about 1 pound) apricot halves, drained
        Raspberry jelly

1. Prepare piecrust mix, following label directions; divide into 8 even pieces.
2. Roll out each on a lightly floured pastry cloth or board to a 5-inch circle; fit into a 3½-inch tart pan; trim edge flush with rim. Prick shells all over with a fork. Place in a large shallow pan for easy handling.
3. Bake in hot oven (425°) 12 minutes, or until golden. Cool completely in pans on wire racks. Remove shells from pans after they have cooled.
4. Combine pudding mix, milk and cream cheese in a medium-size saucepan. Heat slowly, stirring constantly, until cheese melts, then cook, stirring constantly, until mixture thickens and bubbles 1 minute; remove from heat. Pour into a small bowl. Cool, stirring once or twice.
5. Spoon cream mixture into tart shells. Place 1 apricot half, cut side up, on top of each; spoon a rounded teaspoonful of raspberry jelly into each hollow. Chill on a cooky sheet until serving time.

CREAM CHEESE FILLED COFFEECAKE
Serve this warm from the oven or make ahead and reheat some other day.

Bake at 350° for 30 minutes. Makes 2 coffeecakes.

  4¼ cups sifted all-purpose flour
      2 packages active dry yeast
    ¾ cup dairy sour cream
    ½ cup (1 stick) butter, softened
    ¼ cup water
    ½ cup sugar
    ½ teaspoon salt
      1 teaspoon lemon rind
      2 eggs
        Cheese filling (recipe follows)
      1 egg white (from Cheese Filling)
      1 tablespoon sugar (for topping)
    ¼ cup chopped nuts

1. Mix 1½ cups of the flour and undissolved yeast in a large bowl.
2. Combine sour cream, butter, water, sugar, salt and lemon rind together in a small saucepan. Heat until very warm to touch (not scalding), stirring constantly (butter does not have to melt); add to flour mixture with eggs. Beat with electric mixer at low speed ½ minute; then at high speed 3 minutes.
3. Stir in 2 more cups flour to make soft dough.
4. Turn out onto lightly floured pastry board or cloth; knead until smooth and elastic, using remaining flour on board for kneading.
5. When all kneaded in and dough is not sticky (10 minutes), place in a greased large bowl; turn to coat all over; cover with a clean towel. Let rise in warm place, away from draft, 1½ hours, or until double in bulk.
6. While dough rises, make Cheese Filling. Reserve the filling for Step 7.
7. Punch dough down; knead a few times; roll to an 18x16-inch rectangle. Spread evenly with Cheese Filling; roll up, jelly-roll fashion. Cut into two even pieces. Place each half, seam side down, on a lightly greased cooky sheet.
8. Make cuts, 1½ inches apart, along one side of roll from outer edge to center. Repeat on other side, spacing cuts halfway between those on opposite side. Turn each slice slightly on its side. Let rise again, 40 minutes, or until double in bulk. Brush with egg white remaining from Cheese Filling; sprinkle with sugar and nuts.
9. Bake in moderate oven (350°) 30 minutes, or until golden and loaves give a hollow sound when tapped. Remove from cooky sheets to wire racks. Serve while still warm.
10. If made ahead, cake may be reheated, wrapped in foil, in a moderate oven (350°) for 15 minutes.

Cheese Filling: Beat 8 ounces cream cheese, softened; ¼ cup sugar; 1 egg yolk; 1 tablespoon sour cream and ½ teaspoon vanilla until smooth in a small bowl; add ½ cup dark raisins and ½ cup chopped walnuts; stir until mixture is combined.

Left: Fruit and Cheese Fondue is a delightfully easy dessert that's ideal for a company gathering. Recipe is on this page.

SOUR CREAM WALNUT CHEESECAKE

Smaller, yet not less rich than the larger cakes, with a crunchy walnut crust and topping.

Bake at 350° for 40 minutes, then 5 minutes longer to set topping. Makes 12 servings.

    1 cup zwieback crumbs
    2 tablespoons sugar (for crust)
    ¼ cup chopped walnuts
    2 tablespoons butter, melted
    1 pound (16 ounces) cream cheese, softened
    ½ cup sugar
    1 teaspoon vanilla
    3 eggs, well beaten
    1 cup dairy sour cream
    ½ teaspoon vanilla
    1 tablespoon sugar

1. Combine zwieback crumbs, 2 tablespoons sugar and 2 tablespoons of the walnuts; blend in butter. Press mixture evenly on bottom and side of an 8-inch spring-form pan. Chill.
2. Beat cream cheese in large bowl of electric mixer at medium speed until fluffy. Gradually beat in sugar and 1 teaspoon of the vanilla. Beat in eggs, a third at a time. Turn into prepared pan.
3. Bake in moderate oven (350°) 40 minutes, or until center is firm. Remove from oven. Cool on wire rack 5 minutes, away from drafts.
4. Combine sour cream, remaining 1 tablespoon sugar and vanilla. Spread over top of cake; sprinkle with remaining walnuts.
5. Return to moderate oven (350°) for 5 minutes, or until topping is set. Remove from oven; cool in pan on wire rack, away from drafts. Remove side of pan. Refrigerate 4 hours before serving.

WELSH CHEDDAR CHEESECAKE

A surprisingly different cheesecake with the lively tang of Cheddar cheese and beer.

Bake at 475° for 12 minutes, then at 250° for 1½ hours. Makes 16 servings.

    1 box (6 ounces) zwieback crackers, crushed
    3 tablespoons sugar (for crust)
    6 tablespoons (¾ stick) butter, melted
    2 pounds (32 ounces) cream cheese
    8 ounces finely shredded Cheddar cheese (2 cups)
    1¾ cups sugar
    3 tablespoons all-purpose flour
    5 eggs
    3 egg yolks
    ¼ cup beer

1. Combine zwieback crumbs, 3 tablespoons sugar and melted butter in a small bowl. Press firmly over the bottom and partly up the sides of a lightly buttered 9-inch spring-form pan. Chill the crumb crust briefly before filling.
2. Let cream cheese soften in a large bowl. Beat with Cheddar cheese, just until smooth. (Cheeses will beat smoother if they are at room temperature.) Add sugar and flour. Beat until light and fluffy. Add eggs and egg yolks, one at a time, beating well after each addition; stir in beer; pour into crumb crust.
3. Bake in very hot oven (475°) 12 minutes; lower temperature to 250° and bake 1½ hours longer. Turn off oven; let cake remain in oven for an hour.
4. Remove from oven; cool completely on a wire rack; loosen around edge with a knife; release spring and remove side of pan.
Note: It is the nature of this cake to crack on top. However, this will not affect its delicious flavor.

SLIMMED-DOWN LINDY CHEESECAKE

If you love cheesecake but can't afford the calories, try this stingy-on-the-calories version.

Bake at 250° for 1 hour and 10 minutes. Makes 12 servings at 224 calories each.

    1   tablespoon butter
    ½   cup graham cracker crumbs
    1½ pounds (24 ounces) Neufchâtel cheese, softened
    ⅓   cup sugar
        Sugar substitute to equal 6 tablespoons sugar
    1½ tablespoons all-purpose flour
    ¾   teaspoon grated orange rind
    1   teaspoon vanilla
    3   eggs
    1   egg yolk
    2   tablespoons liquid skim milk

1. Butter bottom and side of an 8-inch spring-form pan. Sprinkle with graham cracker crumbs; press firmly into place. Refrigerate 1 hour.
2. Place cheese, sugar, sugar substitute, flour, orange rind, vanilla, eggs, egg yolks and milk in container of electric blender. Whirl 2 minutes, or until mixture is consistency of heavy cream. Spoon gently into pan.
3. Bake in very slow oven (250°) 1 hour and 10 minutes. Turn oven off; open door and allow cheesecake to cool gradually. Refrigerate 4 hours before serving.

LATTICE CHERRY-CHEESE PIE

For a speedy cheese dessert, cover this creamy cheese pie with a sweet cherry topping and bake a cheese lattice on top.

Bake at 350° for 30 minutes, then at 450° for 10 minutes. Makes 8 servings.

    ½   recipe Cooky Crust (recipe on page 135)
    12 ounces cream cheese
    8   ounces cottage cheese
    ¾   cup sugar
    1   teaspoon vanilla
    ⅛   teaspoon ground nutmeg
    2   eggs
    ¼   teaspoon ground cinnamon
    1   can (1 pound, 5 ounces) cherry pie filling

1. Roll out Cooky Crust dough to an 11-inch round on a lightly floured surface, or between 2 sheets of wax paper; fit into a 9-inch pie plate. Trim overhang to ½ inch; turn under, flush with rim.
2. Combine 3 packages of the cream cheese and cottage cheese in medium-size bowl; beat with electric beater until smooth; beat in sugar, vanilla and nutmeg. Add eggs, one at a time, beating well after each; measure out ⅓ cup of mixture; set aside. Pour remaining cheese mixture into prepared pie shell.
3. Bake in moderate oven (350°) 30 minutes. Meanwhile, combine reserved cheese mixture and remaining 1 package cream cheese in bowl; beat until smooth. Fit a pastry bag with a plain round tip (about ¼ inch in diameter); fill with cream-cheese mixture. Stir cinnamon into cherry pie filling.
4. Remove pie from oven; turn oven temperature to 450°. Spread cherry filling over top of pie. Pipe cheese mixture over pie in a lattice pattern and around edge. Bake in very hot oven (450°) 10 minutes longer, or until lattice is nicely browned. Cool completely on wire rack. Serve at room temperature, cut into individual-size wedges.

RICOTTA CHEESE PIE
A fruit-filled Italian cheesecake lightly laced with semisweet chocolate.

Bake at 350° for 1 hour. Makes 8 servings.

1 recipe Cooky Crust (recipe on page 135)
23 ounces ricotta cheese
1⅓ cups sugar
1 tablespoon all-purpose flour
4 eggs, slightly beaten
1 teaspoon vanilla
3 tablespoons semisweet chocolate pieces, coarsely chopped
3 tablespoons candied citron, chopped
3 tablespoons candied orange peel, chopped

1. Roll out half the Cooky Crust dough to a 12-inch round on a lightly floured pastry board; fit into a 9-inch pie plate; trim overhang to ½-inch.
2. Reserve 2 tablespoons egg for brushing pastry later. Combine ricotta cheese, sugar and flour in electric mixer; beat until smooth. Add eggs and vanilla; beat until light and fluffy. Stir in chocolate, citron and orange peel; spoon into prepared pie shell.
3. Roll out remaining Cooky Crust dough to a 12x8-inch rectangle, cut lengthwise into 10 strips with a pastry wheel or knife. Weave strips over filling to make a crisscross top; trim overhang to ½ inch; turn under, flush with rim; flute edge. Mix reserved egg with 1 tablespoon water; brush pastry.
4. Bake in moderate oven (350°) for 1 hour, or until pastry is golden and filling is firm. Cool on wire rack. Sprinkle pie with 10X (confectioners' powdered) sugar and chocolate curls, if you wish.
Note: Check pie after about ½ hour. If edges seem to be getting too brown, cover lightly with aluminum foil for remainder of baking time.

CHIFFON CHEESE TORTE
A surprise blending of cheese and fruits fills fluffy chiffon layers.

Makes 12 servings.

1 packaged lemon or orange chiffon cake (7- to 8-inch diameter)
2 cups (16 ounces) cream-style cottage cheese
½ cup sugar
3 tablespoons chopped mixed candied fruit
1 tablespoon grated orange rind
¼ cup orange juice
1 teaspoon rum extract
2 tablespoons chocolate syrup

1. Place cake on a board. Using a sawing motion with a sharp knife, cut cake into 3 even layers. (You may use your own favorite chiffon cake recipe, if you wish.)
2. In a large bowl of electric mixer, beat cheese at medium speed about 3 minutes, or until smooth; add sugar; beat 2 minutes longer. Stir in candied fruit and orange rind. Combine orange juice and rum extract in a 1-cup measure; reserve.
3. Place bottom layer of cake on serving plate; sprinkle with 5 teaspoons of orange-juice mixture; spread with ⅔ cup of filling; repeat with remaining cake layers, orange-juice mixture and filling, ending with the cheese filling. Chill until serving time.
4. Just before serving, drizzle chocolate syrup over outside edge, letting it run down sides of cake.

CHOCOLATE CHEESECAKE
Cottage cheese takes the spotlight in this rich refrigerator sweet.

Makes 12 to 16 servings.

1 cup chocolate-wafer crumbs
3 tablespoons butter, melted
2 envelopes unflavored gelatin
⅔ cup sugar
2 cups milk
2 eggs, separated
1 package (12 ounces) semisweet chocolate pieces
2 cups cream-style cottage cheese, sieved
1 cup heavy cream

1. Blend chocolate crumbs and butter in a small bowl; press crumb mixture evenly over bottom of a 9-inch spring-form pan.
2. Mix gelatin and ⅓ cup of the sugar in a saucepan; beat in milk and egg yolks. Cook, stirring constantly, until gelatin dissolves; stir in chocolate until melted. Chill 30 minutes; beat in cheese.
3. Beat egg whites until foamy in a small bowl; beat in remaining ⅓ cup sugar until meringue stands in firm peaks. Beat cream until stiff in a bowl. Fold meringue, then cream into chocolate mixture; pour into prepared pan. Chill until firm.

LEMON SWIRL PIE
This 10-minute pie starts with a spicy crumb crust.

Makes 1 eight-inch pie.

- 1 package (5 ounces) shortbread cookies
- 4 tablespoons (½ stick) butter
- 1 teaspoon grated lemon rind
- ¼ teaspoon pumpkin-pie spice
- 8 ounces cream cheese
- 2 cups milk
- 1 package lemon-flavor instant pudding and pie filling mix
- 1 teaspoon vanilla

1. Crush cookies fine. (Tip to speed the job: Place the cookies in a transparent bag, close tightly and roll with a rolling pin.) Measure 2 tablespoons of the cooky crumbs into a cup and set aside for the pie topping in Step 4.
2. Beat butter until soft in a medium-size bowl; blend in remaining crumbs, lemon rind and pumpkin-pie spice. Press evenly over bottom and up side of an 8-inch pie plate. (To shape a stand-up edge, press the cooky crumb mixture between your thumb and forefinger.)
3. Beat cream cheese with ½ cup of the milk until smooth in a medium-size bowl; add remaining milk, instant pudding mix and vanilla; beat with a rotary beater 1 minute, or just until smooth.
4. Spoon into prepared shell. Sprinkle the 2 tablespoons crumbs in a pretty pattern on top. Chill 1 hour, or until firm. Cut in thin wedges.

TRIPLE-CHEESE MOLD WITH STRAWBERRIES
In the French manner, this tangy spread is served with strawberries and crisp crackers.

Makes 8 to 10 servings.

- 8 ounces cream-style cottage cheese
- 1¼ ounces blue cheese
- 8 ounces cream cheese, softened
- 1 cup heavy cream
- 2 teaspoons 10X (confectioners' powdered) sugar
- Dash of salt
- 2 cups (1 pint) strawberries
- Crisp saltines

1. Press cottage cheese and blue cheese through a sieve into a medium-size bowl; blend in cream cheese, cream, 10X sugar and salt until smooth.
2. Cut a piece of double-thick cheesecloth large enough to line a 4-cup mold and cover top; wring out in cold water; line mold. Pack with cheese mixture; fold edge of cloth over top. Turn mold upside down on a wire rack in a shallow pan to catch any liquid that may seep out; chill overnight.
3. When ready to serve, unmold onto a large plate; peel off cheesecloth. Wash but don't hull strawberries; arrange around mold. Serve with saltines.

BABY GOUDA BOWL

Serve this with fruit for dessert, or as part of an appetizer tray: Cut a ½-inch-thick slice across the top of a small Gouda cheese (about 9 ounces) with a very sharp knife. (Cut carefully so as not to break wax edge.) With teaspoon or melon-ball scoop, remove cheese from inside in small petal-like curls. Pile curls back into shell for help-yourself serving.

CHOCOLATE CREAM FROSTING
This recipe makes a rich and creamy frosting.

Makes enough to fill and frost an 8- or 9-inch double-layer cake.

- 8 ounces cream cheese, softened
- 4 tablespoons (½ stick) butter, softened
- 1 package (1 pound) 10X (confectioners' powdered) sugar
- ½ cup dry cocoa
- Dash of salt
- 3 tablespoons milk
- ½ teaspoon vanilla

1. Beat cream cheese and butter until fluffy in a medium-size bowl.
2. Sift 10X sugar, cocoa and salt onto wax paper. Beat into cheese mixture, alternately with milk, until smooth and fluffy; stir in vanilla. Frost cake immediately or store in refrigerator then return to room temperature when ready to use.

DOUBLE APPLE PIE
Cheddar cheese and a lattice pastry top this cider-enriched pie.

Bake at 400° for 45 minutes. Makes 1 nine-inch pie.

- 2 cups cider
- 1 package piecrust mix
- 4 medium-size tart cooking apples, pared, cored, quartered and thinly sliced
- 1 cup firmly packed light brown sugar
- ¼ cup all-purpose flour
- 1 teaspoon apple pie spice
- 1 teaspoon grated lemon rind
- ⅛ teaspoon salt
- 2 tablespoons butter
- 1 tablespoon milk
- 2 teaspoons granulated sugar
- 1½ cups diced Cheddar cheese (6 ounces)

1. Boil cider rapidly in a small saucepan until reduced to ½ cup (about 10 minutes); cool.
2. Prepare piecrust mix, following label directions, or make pastry from your own favorite two-crust recipe. Roll out half to a 12-inch round on a lightly floured pastry cloth or board; fit into a 9-inch pie plate; trim overhang to ½ inch.
3. Combine apples, brown sugar, flour, pie spice,

lemon rind and salt in a large bowl, tossing to coat apple slices evenly. Spoon into pie shell, arranging evenly; dot with butter.

4. Roll out remaining pastry to an 11-inch round; cut strips, ½-inch wide, with a pastry wheel or sharp knife. Weave strips on top of pie to make crisscross top crust; trim ends of strips. Moisten edge of bottom crust; press ends of strips onto bottom crust; flute to make a stand-up edge. Brush strips with milk; sprinkle granulated sugar over top. Carefully pour cider into center of pie.

5. Bake in hot oven (400°) 45 minutes, or until filling bubbles; remove from oven. Place diced cheese in spaces of lattice top.

6. Return to oven for 3 minutes, or just until cheese is melted. Cool on wire rack. For best flavor, serve while pie is still slightly warm.

ROYAL CHOCOLATE CREAM
Each spoonful of this luscious cream-cheese "soufflé" tempts you to have just one more bite.

Makes 8 servings.

    ¾ cup firmly packed light brown sugar
    1 envelope unflavored gelatin
    ½ cup water
    1 cup semisweet-chocolate pieces
    4 eggs, separated
    8 ounces cream cheese
    1 teaspoon vanilla
    1½ cups heavy cream

1. Prepare a 4-cup soufflé or straight-side baking dish this way: Cut a strip of foil 12 inches wide and long enough to go around dish with a 1-inch overlap; fold in half lengthwise. Wrap around dish to make a 2-inch stand-up collar; hold in place with a rubber band and a paper clip.

2. Mix ¼ cup of the brown sugar with gelatin in the top of a double boiler. Stir in water and semisweet-chocolate pieces.

3. Heat, stirring constantly, over simmering water 10 minutes, or until gelatin dissolves and chocolate melts completely.

4. Beat egg yolks slightly in a bowl; slowly stir in about half of the hot chocolate mixture, then stir back into remaining mixture in top of double boiler. Cook, stirring constantly, over simmering water 3 minutes; remove from heat.

5. Beat cream cheese until soft in a large bowl; slowly beat in chocolate mixture until smooth; stir in vanilla. Chill just until mixture is as thick as unbeaten egg white.

6. While gelatin mixture chills, beat egg whites until foamy-white and double in volume in a medium-size bowl; beat in remaining ½ cup brown sugar, 1 tablespoon at a time, until meringue forms soft peaks. Beat 1 cup of the cream until stiff in a second medium-size bowl.

7. Beat gelatin mixture until fluffy-light. Fold in meringue, then whipped cream until no streaks of

white remain; spoon into prepared dish. Chill several hours, or until firm.

8. When ready to serve, beat remaining ½ cup cream until stiff in a small bowl. Remove foil collar from soufflé; spoon whipped cream in poufs on top. Serve immediately.

PLUM ROLL ROYALE
This lightly spiced cake has a filling of cream and cottage cheeses, plum slices and lemon.

Bake at 400° for 15 minutes. Makes 8 servings.

    ¾ cup sifted cake flour
    1 teaspoon baking powder
    ¼ teaspoon salt
    ¼ teaspoon ground cinnamon
    ⅛ teaspoon ground nutmeg
    4 eggs
    ¾ cup granulated sugar
    ½ teaspoon vanilla
    3 or 4 ounces cream cheese
    1 cup (8 ounces) cream-style cottage cheese
    ½ cup 10X (confectioners' powdered) sugar
    1 tablespoon lemon juice
    8 medium-size ripe red plums, halved, pitted and
       sliced thin (2 cups)

1. Grease a jelly-roll pan, 15x10x1; line with wax paper; grease paper.

2. Measure flour, baking powder, salt and spices into sifter.

3. Beat eggs until foamy in a large bowl; slowly beat in granulated sugar until creamy-thick; stir in vanilla. Sift flour mixture over top, then fold in. Pour into prepared pan, spreading evenly.

4. Bake in hot oven (400°) 15 minutes, or until center springs back when lightly pressed with fingertip.

5. Invert cake onto a towel sprinkled with 10X sugar; remove pan; peel off wax paper. Trim crisp edges from cake. Starting at one end, roll cake, jelly-roll fashion; wrap in towel; cool cake completely before adding the filling.

6. Beat cream cheese with cottage cheese, then ½ cup 10X sugar and lemon juice until fluffy in a medium-size bowl.

7. Unroll cake; spread with cheese mixture; arrange plum slices in a single layer on top. Reroll cake. Chill at least two hours.

QUICK FRUIT AND CHEESE DESSERT

Chill 8 ounces cream cheese until firm enough to handle, then cut crosswise into sixths and lengthwise into quarters to make 24 pieces; press a pecan half into top of each. Crush enough graham crackers to measure ½ cup crumbs; mix with 1 tablespoon sugar and ¼ teaspoon cinnamon in a pie plate. Roll cheese rectangles into crumb mixture to coat well; chill again. Serve with assorted cut fruits for dessert. Makes 24 rectangles.

INDEX

BUYER'S GUIDE

Page 39: Wood bed tray from Robert Webb, Inc., 900 First Ave., New York, N. Y. 10022; "Kosta" bud vase #46245 from Georg Jensen, Inc., 601 Madison Ave., New York, N. Y. 10022; Lady Pepperell sheets from WestPoint Pepperell, 1221 Avenue of the Americas, New York, N. Y. 10020; "Danish Inn" goblet by Holme Gaard of Copenhagen, available at Royal Copenhagen, 573 Madison Ave., New York, N. Y. 10022; "Domino" porcelain creamer, sugar bowl with lid, tea cup and saucer, bread and butter plate by Royal Copenhagen Porcelain, available at Royal Copenhagen, 573 Madison Ave., New York, N. Y.
Page 48: Butler tray from Lucidity, 755 Madison Ave., New York, N. Y. 10021.
Page 50: Buffet tray from Hammacher Schlemmer, 147 East 57th St., New York, N.Y. 10022.
Pages 84-85: "Kingdom of the Sea" china by Portmeirion, available at Bloomingdale's, 1000 Third Ave., New York, N. Y. 10022; "Danish Inn" claret and white wine glasses by Holme Gaard of Copenhagen, available at Royal Copenhagen, 573 Madison Ave., New York, N. Y.

PHOTOGRAPHS

Photographs by George Nordhausen except the following:
Gordon Smith, pages 2, 5, 7, 9, 12-13, 16-17, 36-37, 100-101 and 116-117.
Philip Sykes, pages 20-21, 24, 48, 60-61 and 132-133.

The editor gratefully acknowledges the cooperation of the Wright Brothers Farm in Lagrangèville, New York for the photographs appearing on pages 2, 100-101 and 116-117; and of The Big Cheese, Jane St., New York, N. Y., for the photograph on page 5.

ILLUSTRATIONS

Adolph Brotman, pages 18, 27, 35, 38 and 74.
Joseph Patti, pages 4, 19, 33, 51, 71, 91, 109, 121 and 131.